People: The Real Business of Leadership

Release the Amazing Power of People through Service, Respect and the Inclusive Culture!

By

Michael T. Baker

Copyright © 2010 Michael T. Baker

ISBN 978-1-60910-161-9

All rights reserved. No part of this publication may be reproduced, stored in a retrieval system, or transmitted in any form or by any means, electronic, mechanical, recording or otherwise, without the prior written permission of the author.

Printed in the United States of America.

BookLocker.com, Inc.
2010

Dedication

This book is dedicated to my father, E.R. "Russ" Baker, who taught me throughout his lifetime the power of people and their capacity to accomplish amazing things when given the opportunity to be included, heard, and respected.

Acknowledgements

For Joan, whose love and support is the foundation of our home, faith and happiness. For Brett and Stacy who have shared their professional expertise with love and a healthy dose of common sense. For Mom, whose "to thine own self be true" counsel followed me into every company meeting. I love you all and thank you for the constant reminder that people make the difference.

Thanks to all my family, friends, colleagues, managers, staff, and the guys and gals in the plants whose hard work, contributions, and support made me look good, always better than I deserved.

I also want to thank my editor, Harvey Stanbrough, for his professionalism, skill, and style. Harvey gave my rambling ideas structure and flow, allowing the reader to find the real essence of people's capacity to contribute.

To Angela Hoy, Todd Engel and the wonderful staff at BookLocker.com, thank you for your honest, open approach to publishing. You made it possible for me to share a message on the passion and power of people.

Table of Contents

Introduction 1
Chapter 1: The Foundation of Leadership 5
Chapter 2: Foundation Principles 9
Chapter 3: The Core Beliefs 19
Chapter 4: The Culture 26
Chapter 5: The Culture You Have Now 29
Chapter 6: The Culture You Want 36
Chapter 7: How Do We Get There? 40
Chapter 8: The Manager and the Work 45
Chapter 9: The "mSt" Model 49
Chapter 10: m — The Mechanical Element 51
Chapter 11: t — The Technical Element 56
Chapter 12: S - The Social Element 63
Chapter 13: The Segments of Work (The Issue Map) 68
Chapter 14: The Manager Tools 76
Chapter 15: The "9:30 Meeting" 77
Chapter 16: Site Communication Meetings 81
Chapter 17: The Visual Site 85
Chapter 18: 5S 91
Chapter 19: The Visual Manager 93
Chapter 20: Management Review 96
Chapter 21: Building and Managing Labor Relations 103
Chapter 22: The Site Manager and the Local Union
    President 106

Chapter 23: The Department Manager and the
   Committee Rep 110
Chapter 24: The Supervisor and the Shift Steward 113
Chapter 25: The Working-Together Platform (Joint Leadership
   Meetings) 117
Chapter 26: Human Resources and the Union 122
Chapter 27: Human Resources in the Inclusive Culture 124
Chapter 28: The Power of People 136
Bibliography 139

Introduction

After 10 years as a teacher-coach, followed by 25 years in industrial manufacturing, I retired at the end of the year. It was not so much a retirement as a change in direction, a next chapter, predicated on the belief that I had something to share. My experiences, successes and failures, had brought me to this point. Every job in the previous 35 years had prepared me for this new direction. I founded Michael T. Baker, LLC for the purpose of sharing my management and leadership theories with anyone who would listen. This was not an easy decision but one I made with confidence. It was simply time to move on, and with the developing economic meltdown occurring, it was the right time for this message.

Throughout my career, I've had the opportunity to study and learn from managers with a variety of leadership styles. My career has been based on the idea that leadership is service and people are, in fact, our most valuable resource. In order to effectively lead, one must be willing to serve and one must be willing to develop an inclusive culture in order to optimize people's impact. The authority vested in a leadership role requires one to offer the invitation to contribute. This is a common-sense premise based in the idea that the best chance of success occurs when all the resources of an organization are engaged, included, and respected. It requires a belief that the very authority of the role also empowers one to affect the quality of life for others. I also believe that impact on quality of life can and will affect the success of the business. I believe that effect is universal and applicable to any organization, institution, or business.

With all our technological advancement, process development, and scientific understanding, the differentiation is still embedded in the people of the organization. A great deal of lip service is given to this idea but the question remains: How effectively are we utilizing people beyond typical measurements of productivity, behavioral expectations, and turnover? Do our policies, systems, styles, and organizational cultures tap into the best instincts of our employees, and in turn optimize our organizational performance? The answer is no, certainly not as effectively as we think they do.

In a variety of management roles in the aluminum manufacturing industry, I was able to test those very questions, methods, and beliefs. Although measurements and processes were different, the people responded in strikingly similar ways. Regardless of role or level in the organization, people want good leadership. People want sincerity, respect, and inclusion. When we create and nurture the environment for those attributes, dramatic change occurs and powerful outcomes follow.

There are hundreds of books, studies, and papers on the virtues of documented management styles. Those all explore in scientific terms the characteristics, impact, and predicted results, complete with case studies. Most were written by experts, gurus, and business school professors and nearly all are acclaimed by the business community. I make no attempt to refute those works. I state my ideas and beliefs on the basis of three decades of leading real people in real work situations with daily accountability for results. I had numerous failures but more successes, and I hold a continuing belief that the exponential power of people, given effective leadership in an inclusive culture, will trump the academic study.

Does the leadership style of your organization provide a platform for that exponential power?

PEOPLE: THE REAL BUSINESS OF LEADERSHIP

This book will attempt to capture the last 35 years of lessons learned about the power of people and the impact of an inclusive culture. If people are our most valuable resource, we must nurture a culture that values the passion, creativity and spirit of people. Those are lessons worth sharing.

It will outline the beliefs, tools, and possibilities of what impact we have on our employees' quality of life and the resulting impact they will have on our businesses.

The current economic times suggest the bubble has burst. Unchecked growth, expansion, and spending have resulted in heavy corporate and personal debt that, in many cases, is backed only by exotic swaps and financial instruments unable to withstand the dramatic market correction and are fueling the resulting global recession. The result has been the wholesale jettison of jobs. Jobs are done by people. Taking their job also takes their income, their pride and, in many cases, their way of life.

The world is changing. By necessity, back to basics is the new way. Greed is not an admirable personality trait and materialism is not the lifestyle strategy of the day. Nearly everyone is being forced to redefine their priorities and values. Millions are out of work and find themselves in career centers and in technical and community colleges, redefining and retraining themselves. Many will flourish in this new environment and will find their true calling. Many will struggle and find added frustration as they search for new skills and talents that simply don't exist. Those will be left hoping the economy and their jobs recover. Good leadership, or the lack of it, will play a critical role in the degree of recovery and in the restoration and creation of jobs.

Nearly all experts agree the economy will recover. When it will recover and how many jobs will be restored and how many new jobs will be created, nobody knows. How will we as leaders and managers respond, not only to the challenges of this economic crisis but also to the recovery and rebuilding of our businesses and industries? This is the time to rethink our values, our cultures, and our passions. It is time to redefine our idea of leadership and how we truly view people, our most valuable resource.

If the concept of "leadership is service" is a new idea, it is an idea whose time has come. If the idea is not new, I believe it is time to renew our belief in the power of people in our businesses and organizations. It is time to redefine the essence of leadership. The 10% unemployed, their families, and the bankrupt, failed, and dying businesses would suggest that whatever we're doing now isn't working.

Chapter 1:
The Foundation of Leadership

The core of any organization is its people. People are referred to as "assets," "resources," and the all time favorite "FTEs." Full time employees (FTEs) are our most expensive asset, and invariably, the one we always have too many of, or so we are told. FTE is a convenient acronym, sounds very clinical and works well when considering downsizing, layoffs, restructures, or just plain old getting rid of people. As managers, we've all done it, and we've all had to do it. It's not an easy task but somehow it seems easier when we are working with FTEs instead of HBs, human beings.

Industry and business have always gone through transformations. At one time a popular solution was to throw people at the problem. With enough resources, we had a better chance of solving problems, finding better technology, and overcoming the competition. We could add another production line, another shift or create another department to deal with specific issues. This worked in many cases but obviously created higher fixed costs and required more capital. When the market recedes and margins slide, we scramble to reduce those costs and have to let people go. This, of course, creates another layer of costs in unemployment benefits, training liabilities, and dormant or sub-utilized equipment and capital.

The other result of lay-offs is the cost to the business in terms of quality, overtime, morale, and recovery. Don't misunderstand: reduction of force is sometimes essential to the survival of a business, and in many instances, is just the prelim to the eventual failure of a business. However, I submit that we must analyze carefully how we expand our business and how we make additions to the resources, both human and physical capital.

Attempt growth too quickly or add resources without careful analysis, and the business cannot respond and support the cost. So the remedy becomes extreme downsizing in order to survive. What appears to the newly hired to have been an answered prayer now becomes a severe injustice. And we must analyze, just as carefully, how we reduce those resources. The cost, on all fronts, is simply too high.

When I accepted the role of general manager of a large manufacturing plant in 2001, there were 188 production employees on lay-off. Over the course of the following year, business strengthened, and we began the recall of those employees. Studying the data over the next two years, I found that it took the plant close to 18 months to rebound to the quality and productivity levels prior to the lay-off. Employees returning after their lengthy furloughs were bumped through the job grades to return to their incumbent jobs. The training liability to the plant was enormous, pushing overtime cost 20-30% higher. The internal rejection rate more than doubled as people re-learned their jobs. At that point, I concluded there had to be a better way.

When business cycled down again in late 2003, the call came again for a reduction. I resisted a lay-off and proposed reducing the four-day shift to a three-day shift. This would keep the shifts and crews intact but would reduce the output of the plant and take a 12 hour day out of all employees' schedules. This, along with a shutdown of certain equipment, reduced maintenance costs, supply costs, and energy costs and payroll. It also allowed us to reduce operating costs by 40% over a 5 month period, and it created a good-will culture among all the employees and paid productivity, quality and cost dividends in the years to come.

As this unprecedented economic crisis has unfolded, I've wondered what the impact would be if more companies took that approach before reducing jobs. And hopefully, many are looking at options prior to layoffs. With over 7 million jobs lost through November of 2009, what percentage could have been saved or what would be the financial impact with more of those people still working?

Although many of the job losses reflected a survival move by their company, how many companies could have afforded to take a temporary reduction or adjustment in profitability and keep some portion of the employees working? If a company is going under, certainly it must take whatever action is necessary to survive, but if a company can survive, remain financially viable, and lay off fewer employees, isn't that a worthy action that might shorten the recession? I'm not an economist, but common sense tells me that if we keep more people and families eating out, buying washers and dryers, TV's, and cars, we will get on the road to recovery sooner. What if every company that could, hired back 10% of the workers that were laid off within the last 12 months? What financial impact would that have on the spending issue of this crisis?

One could argue about the elements of the union contract that required a seniority-based job bump or other contractual elements that historically are attributed to cost additions. In a union facility, the reality is that there is a contract and it is what it is. Although your objectives may be to negotiate specific changes, you have what you have today. This book will deal with how you can make cultural change and operational effectiveness within your current union status.

As previously stated, the core of any organization is its people. On financial statements the company assets are stated in objective numeric terms. They are represented by property, cash, equipment and other financial holdings.

Although many companies refer to their employees as their most valuable asset, it is always interesting to get the employees view on that claim. The business world today is in constant change, ruthlessly competitive on many levels, and financially unforgiving. The environment implies a tough, no-nonsense approach to survival and profitability.

Each organization defines success with different metrics. Those metrics require individual and team performance to achieve sustained and "heroic" gains. People-centered and service-based leadership is a valid pathway to achieving and sustaining both the gains and profitability in an increasingly tougher and more impersonal business environment.

Chapter 2:
Foundation Principles

Past and present leadership books refer to the characteristics of an effective leader. Honesty, sincerity, initiative, enthusiasm, passion, and assertiveness, among others, are essential to being an effective leader and manager. In addition, I've come to believe in five foundations, which I formulated over the years and are tried and true.

I. Lead from a position of service. As the general manager of a large manufacturing plant, I quickly learned the buck stopped here. For that facility, I was the last word, I had the accountability, and I had to make the final decisions. I understood the authority vested in this role also carried a responsibility and a consequence for those decisions.

As the GM, I was the steward of the company's assets; physical, technical, and human. I knew the business, our processes, the strengths and weakness of the facility, our position in the industry, and our level of competition. I knew the measurements of the business and how success was defined. I knew the capabilities of our resources, the constraints of our capital availability, and the areas requiring both incremental and heroic improvement. I was fully aware of the expectations of our executives and the company's expectations of me and the facility. Those were tangible, documented, and measurable against standards within the plant, the company, and our industry.

The physical and the technical requirements were covered. The physical plant was a 40 year old manufacturing facility with typical aging infrastructure issues. However, it was well equipped and had the technology and processes in order to be competitive. We had very skilled and experienced employees in every department from the production, maintenance, and engineering disciplines.

The human element would be the deciding factor, our edge over the competition, the difference between good and great, the difference between incremental and heroic gains. If we found the right button, created the right environment, and built a culture of inclusiveness, the organization would be different and it would change lives.

Leading from a position of service requires first and foremost the elimination of ego, but not all ego because one necessary characteristic of effective leadership is confidence. People have to sense it and see it in their leaders. Certainly there is a difference between ego and confidence. Drop the ego, be confident in your beliefs and your actions, and people will follow. Combine the vested authority of the role with a passion for service and powerful things will happen. It will change how people think, how they act, and how they approach their jobs, and it will change their lives. In turn, they will positively affect the business.

Service implies a genuine attempt to make decisions that not only positively affect the business but people's work life. All things being equal, does this decision advance the culture of the organization? Is there some impact of this issue that, if handled differently, will make a difference? Many times, those situations affect only one employee at a time. My experience has been that in those circumstances, the individual becomes an ambassador for the culture change.

During our annual Christmas dinner we served over 800 employees a dinner of ham and turkey with all the fixings. We did this in the large training room with music playing and decorations. The cost was minimal but it sent a strong message to the workforce. During those dinners, as the plant manager, I would grab a large tray of rolls and wander among the tables, serving extra dinner rolls. It was a small gesture but it had a huge impact. The plant manager of the facility was literally serving the workforce at the Christmas dinner. It made a difference in how I was perceived and it generated a level of respect outside the formal vested authority of the role.

The open door policy, the communication meetings, and the appropriate follow up to questions and concerns all can have the feel of service. The workforce will sense a genuine effort to be a resource for the employees, not just a boss.

Donald T. Phillips, in his book, Lincoln on Leadership, wrote of his own experiences after researching Lincoln's particular brand of leadership: "Having been in the business world for many years now, mostly in large corporate settings, I am still confounded and amazed that, of the hundreds of managers and supervisors I've encountered, I can count on one hand the number of real leaders among them."

It's unfortunate, but I agree with Mr. Phillips. Being in charge does not make an effective leader. Again, it starts with a genuine desire to be of service to your people and your company. They go hand in hand.

II. Genuinely care about people. This foundation goes with the idea of service. I believe it's impossible to have one without the other. The very premise of leadership implies the desire to have an impact on people and their actions. The young manager, when asked how he liked his new job, replied, it would be great if I didn't have all those people problems. How true and how sad this sentiment is, and how widespread. People are the business of leadership. Management is the oversight of a process that happens to involve people. Leadership is about touching something in people that stirs action, positive action that affects the organization and changes outcomes. If you don't care for people, enjoy the interaction, welcome the challenge of interaction, and have a <u>need</u> to improve your people's situation, you will have difficulty being effective in a leadership role.

This principle goes deeper than the traditional idea of liking someone. No doubt, people can be difficult and they come in all shapes, sizes and personalities. It's not practical that, as leaders, we personally like everyone in our organization. This principle simply suggests that effective leadership begins with a desire to work with, motivate, and help people achieve positive results in their lives.

Many organizations are larger than their surrounding communities and towns. As communities are composed of different personalities and characters, good and bad, so it is with organizations. Our hiring practices, systems, and methods do not guarantee we bring only the best of the best into our organizations. We strive for that, but the human factor will ensure that we always get a cross section of personalities and capabilities. As sophisticated as our hiring systems are, many times, we rely on our instincts about people to make the final decision. Understanding the differences in personalities, adjusting our approach, and recognizing people's strengths and weaknesses can determine our effectiveness and our outcomes. My father, who was in management with General Electric for 35 years, once told me, "Son, any fool can fire somebody. It takes a real leader to make a weak employee a good employee." I never forgot that, and in the many cases throughout my career where termination was the solution, I always tried to make it as timely and as wisely as possible and only after all other reasonable attempts had failed. Of course, termination is a reality and a necessary action, but the replacement cost alone should be motivation enough to attempt behavior or performance change where possible.

As managers and leaders, we've all been in the position of being confronted by a concerned or troubled employee. In either a one-on-one or group situation, an employee venting his frustration or anger can be a daunting situation. People have different capabilities in expressing themselves, presenting their case, and communicating emotional issues. The best advice I received on this issue came from a senior manager who told me to "focus on the message and not on the package." That was exactly the right tactic. It also occurred to me that, many times, the frustration, anger and emotion were part of the package because no one was listening. How many times had this employee expressed the same issue to other leaders in the department? With no follow up or satisfaction that the issue was taken seriously, the employee kept going up the ladder to get someone to listen. By the time he got to me, he it was frustrated and angry. So the package was not pretty. The message was the issue, but it was wrapped in a package of frustration, neglect, and anger. As effective leaders, we must look beyond the package and focus on the message.

If people are the problem and they take your time and sap your energy, then I suggest you might be missing opportunities to optimize the performance of your organization. In this case, the leadership becomes process based, data based, and a "paint by numbers" style. This promotes a culture and style that views every issue and decision as a formula. When worked like a math equation, some believe a formula will yield the best solution. Maybe, maybe not. In this environment, incremental gains can certainly be achieved. Marginal or poor leaders want a quick solution. They want to see a step-by-step or paint-by-numbers approach to solving issues. They want to avoid the discretionary and sometimes risky element of actual decision making. The essence of effective leadership is embracing the time and energy to make decisions based not only on the data and the facts, but also on the impact of and the impact on people. This requires a genuine caring for people.

III. "Do the Right Thing" is always the basis. This is an overused idea and always the objective. It's one of those ideas that are easy to say but sometimes difficult to do. As managers and leaders, we want to do the right thing. Although there are certainly unscrupulous and mean-spirited managers in some organizations, more common are people in those roles who genuinely want to do it right. This concept becomes a platform from which we, as managers, can measure each issue and evaluate each potential solution. If we start here, the rest, although not necessarily easier, is clearer.

My approach with employees, staff, and union leadership was based on the idea that, whatever the issue, we would always try to do the right thing. The solution or outcome would not be based on union membership, role in the organization, what we'd always done, or any other preconceived factors. We'd look at the facts of the issue, and together, we'd try to determine the right thing to do.

Within any organization, there are multiple issues and factors that must be considered in all situations. No one area of the facility or business can effectively be managed in a vacuum. There is truth in the old saying that if you pull on one end of the rope, the other end will invariably move. Every action has a reaction. One area of performance comes to mind. Management of safety in a facility is dependent on many variables. Certainly employee behavior is critical, as in consistently wearing proper personal protective equipment as well as proactively considering safety factors prior to performing a job. There are also other considerations, such as perception, past practices, and engineering and equipment design issues that must be considered as the safety program is designed, implemented and enforced. Safety, as a behavioral and performance element, exists as part of the overall facility culture. It is critical to understand this as one manages the safety program. It doesn't dictate that you don't take certain actions or make certain decisions; it simply requires an understanding of the potential outcomes and results while considering solutions.

Also, it's important to understand that the definition of "right thing" is not always a black and white issue. It means different things to different people and could have different contexts within a particular organization. The effective leader must understand this variable and consider legacy issues, facility history, and current perceptions.

Doing the right thing must be viewed by others in the organization as a characteristic of the leader. This is demonstrated by a pattern of responses, decisions, and outcomes. No one is perfect and no one will make the right decision in every case, and truthfully, no one expects that of anyone in any capacity. What is expected is that the leader's demonstrated behavior over time gives assurance to the organization that doing the right thing will always be the objective and the desired outcome. When this assurance occurs, trust is the starting point of any discussion or problem-solving event. With trust, relationships in the organization mature to levels that make powerful outcomes possible, and that is a competitive edge in any business.

IV. Believe that people affect the organization. Capital can purchase state-of-the-art equipment, the latest technology, and upgraded processes. Systems can be refined and upgraded to provide the best opportunity for success. Only people remain the constant variable in any organization's success. I've heard it said that the factory of the future will have two employees: a man and a dog. The man's job will be to feed the dog and the dog's job will be to keep the man from touching anything. That's an interesting concept, especially in this intelligent-computer age. The technology is amazing and is advancing on a daily basis. However, until that time when everything is automated, people remain essential.

Walk into any organization and ask a group of employees how many said, when asked at graduation from high school, that they wanted to be doing what they're doing today. For most people, the job they're in today is not what they planned. It was not their dream. But here they are because of decisions they made along the way. They made some decisions at their discretion, and in some they had little or no choice. Perhaps they were in college when a parent became ill and their dream had to be put on hold or was permanently ended. Perhaps they got careless, got into trouble, and watched from the sideline as their dream vanished. We are the product of the decisions we make.

Whatever their road to the present situation, here they are, and most are working hard, making the best of the situation. Many are working well below their capabilities and each day can be a monotonous struggle. The frustration of working below one's potential is real and it occurs every day in businesses and industries everywhere. One's specific role in the organization does not always reflect the intellectual and creative talents of the person. I've known fork truck drivers in the plant who had the mental and emotional intelligence and natural abilities of the CEO and other high-level executives. Again, for a variety of reasons, one individual ends up in an executive role while another is in a role of lesser accountability.

One of leadership's greatest challenges is to find ways to tap the knowledge, experience and natural abilities of the workforce. It is difficult to change the basic nature of a repetitive and tedious production-line job. It is difficult and many times not practical or productive to broaden processes to allow creative variations in the job. The product quality and consistency demands process integrity and repetition.

The effective leader can do two things to engage employees in this situation: First, the leader must be alert to recognize those employees with potential greater than their current role. The leader must consistently interact with and challenge the employee to consider taking on more expanded roles in the organization. Second, the leader must build and nurture an inclusive culture in the organization. There must be a natural tendency to bring people into the process, and not just on occasion when there is a need for committees, teams, and special projects. Those are critical and must have representation from different employee groups, but also there must be the consistent conversation, communication that allows the employee to feel he is part of the solution and a valued contributor to the overall success of the organization.

People, regardless of job, title, or salary, want to be part of something important. Most employees have a desire and a need to contribute and add value, and everyone has a need to feel important. As effective leaders, we must tap into that need, find ways to help people feel important, feel valued, and make positive contributions. As leaders, we have many opportunities throughout our day to interact and touch the right buttons in our employees. I often told young supervisors and managers to think of it this way: when your employees go home and sit at the dinner table with their families, when their son or daughter asks them, "Daddy, what did you do at work today?" how they answer that question will depend on how you did your job today. Did you help foster an environment in which the employee felt valued, made a contribution, and made a difference? Who among us, regardless of our job, title, or salary, does not want our children to be proud of us and what we do? I submit that, as a leader, you have the ability to help people meet that basic need. In turn, they will help you, and powerful things will begin to happen in your organization. People do have an impact. As an effective leader, your job is to ensure it's a positive and powerful impact.

V. Impact is a valid pathway to success. This concept simply confirms the belief that an inclusive culture allowing all employees to contribute in a positive, meaningful way will create a powerful impact on the organization. The impact of individual employees is a valid pathway to profitability, productivity, and differentiation from competitors. Most organizations will proclaim to accept the value of its employees and attempt to provide a culture that allows participation and contribution. The question is not the attempt or intention, but the execution and sustainability of those values. Many times those values are mandated or embedded in the company's mission or vision statements, policies and systems. They can be referenced and articulated, but are they visible and internalized within the behavior and style of the leadership in the organization? Left to gather dust in a policy handbook or on a bulletin board, such values yield few or no results. They must be instinctive to the effective leader and lived every day.

The effective leader possesses many characteristics necessary to gain credibility and respect, and to affect behavior. In addition, if the work comes from a perspective of service to people who are genuinely cared for with an attempt to do the right thing, positive changes and powerful outcomes will occur when all employees feel they can positively affect the organization.

Chapter 3:
The Core Beliefs

The foundations in chapter 1 are the values that provide the platform for the effective leader to approach their work and their employees. Those values lay the groundwork of trust and credibility. Without trust and credibility, the message is not received. The opportunity for heroic gains never materializes and, at best, a steady status quo will be the trademark of the organization.

I tried to incorporate three core beliefs in my management and leadership career. I used those beliefs to filter my decisions, my actions, and my interaction with everyone in the organization. They helped define how I approached problems, how I assigned work, and how I viewed the resources available. Combined with the foundations discussed earlier, those core beliefs provided the basis of an inclusive culture.

I. It's amazing what can be accomplished when you don't care who gets the credit. You don't have to have all the answers. Recognizing one's strengths is essential, but recognizing one's weaknesses is critical. Ego is the great disabler of effective leadership. As I mentioned earlier, confidence, assertiveness, and aggressiveness are essential to the effective leader. Ego, unchecked, will derail the effort and demoralize and alienate others. That alienation will dilute the cumulative power and strength of the organization and kill possibilities for greater success. In such an environment, people will find their comfort zone and resort to the lowest common denominator of productivity and contribution.

A simple concept but one that is too often overlooked, is that people want to add value, contribute and be recognized. When people know the culture allows contribution and recognition, they will look for ways to improve the business. Those concepts also assume a belief that most people want to do the right thing and take pride in doing a good job. When you examine your workforce, I believe you'll find it to be universal. Most people want to raise their children, support their family and live the American dream. Create the environment and give credit where credit's due and watch what happens.

This approach also has tangible benefits to the business. When the environment supports a structure that limits employees to specific areas of impact, we lose opportunities to improve. Of course, there must be structure and clearly defined role accountabilities—without it, there would be organized chaos and few decisions would be made—however, we will optimize the organization's potential if we develop systems and cultures that allow a variety of contributions by the workforce.

One example I've seen is the working relationship between shift supervisors and the union's shift steward. Assigning overtime is primarily the domain of the shift supervisor, but it's also an area where the most grievances are filed by the employees. Those grievances are based on the belief that mistakes have been made and employees have been deprived of overtime. Many times the supervisor is charged with partiality or just doesn't properly interpret the contractual rules. Those grievances, when upheld, allow for the wronged employee to be granted the missed overtime pay or a bump up in the line for the next overtime.

Whatever the result, the entire process can be inefficient, time consuming, expensive, and the source of ill-will and unproductive perceptions. Often the culture dictates that the supervisor is accountable for the process, and bringing the union steward into the process is neither suggested nor condoned. To do so would indicate weakness on the part of management, or "allowing the fox in the hen house." But I suggest this is <u>exactly</u> the right thing to do. By working together, there is ownership in the process with the union and collaboration on the contract interpretation. The result will be fewer mistakes, fewer grievances, and more productive use of everyone's time. This builds an inclusive culture and pays dividends throughout the business. The credit goes to all involved.

In today's competitive environment, we cannot afford to let ego, pride, or territorial lines prevent us from utilizing all our experienced resources to gain a competitive edge. When you don't care who gets the credit, powerful things can happen.

<u>II. Nothing is impossible if you don't have to do it.</u> As managers and leaders, we must have a vision of the organization's goals and objectives. That vision is then translated into assigned tasks with specific expected outcomes and results. With the proper structure and capable resources, the organization works to meet and exceed those objectives.

Effective leadership sets attainable expectations while challenging all resources to achieve the results. A popular trend has been to also define "stretch" goals. Those super goals are intended to obtain effort greater than needed to achieve the original goals, but they often result in frustration and disappointment when only the primary objective is achieved. In my view, this practice is counterproductive. If we have good analysis up front and effective implementation, and if we achieve the established objectives, we can then re-calibrate and move to the next level.

Many times in our efforts to assign work or set expectations, we lose sight of the constraints and limitations of both the people and the organization. We begin to mandate results, task without proper analysis of capabilities and still expect results. This is the essence of "nothing is impossible if you don't have to do it." Our role as managers is to assess the strength and weaknesses of the organization and ensure we have the proper resources in place. Our team, our equipment, our systems and processes all must be properly evaluated before we can expect success. If not, we set up people and processes to fail. Failure may be defined as simply maintaining the status quo. Failure may also come as a result of the paralysis many experience when feeling overwhelmed. People will find the boundaries quickly and will learn to survive within those boundaries. The businesses making the heroic gains in today's challenging environment are not the ones simply living within the boundaries. Engaged, energized, enabled and passionate employees live outside the boundaries and make powerful things happen.

This does not mean we shouldn't challenge our employees. Challenging people to reach beyond their typical effort or capabilities is critical to success and differentiation in a very competitive global market. I simply suggest that this challenge must come only after careful analysis of our resource capabilities. Internalizing the idea that "nothing is impossible if you don't have to do it" keeps up grounded in our expectations and ensures we are making continued progress in our work to optimize our organizations.

III. The authority vested in a leadership role requires offering the invitation to contribute.

A management or leadership role is accountable for the culture, output, and success of the organization. Managers make daily decisions that define the culture, set policy, and determine how the organization does business. This culture can be one of command and control, allowing only a handful of executives to make decisions, or it can be an inclusive culture that draws on the experience and capabilities of all the resources available. The "leave your brain at the gate" mentality doesn't work, certainly not in today's extreme competitive environment. It's a flagrant waste of capability, opportunity, and money.

Every organization has both formal and informal leaders. The formal leaders have the authority vested in the role they occupy, but informal leaders have authority vested in the relationships, respect, and trust of their fellow employees. The work of every manager-leader should be to recognize and identify those individuals within the organization. Informal leaders can affect and influence the culture in both a positive and negative way. The smart manager will utilize those individuals to advance the organization's objectives and improve facility performance.

Although many employees will recognize opportunities to improve processes, systems and cultures, they will, in most cases, be limited to how much impact they can have. If improvements or cultural changes are initiated by employees, those changes may not be sustainable or may have limited impact. True and sustainable change occurs only when management authorizes the change.

When employees feel they are operating in unauthorized systems or processes, they will find their boundaries and contribution will be limited, at best.

Simply put, in an inclusive culture, the invitation to contribute is an integral part of the manager-employee interaction. It is the norm, not the exception. It is the day-to-day communication that allows all employees to freely offer suggestions for improvements, engage in problem solving, and routinely contribute to the success of the facility. Management must formally offer this invitation and make it part of the facility culture. The return in contribution, trust, and heroic gains will be powerful and continuous.

Recognizing credit for success, understanding constraints and capabilities, and nurturing a culture of contribution will create a platform for achieving unlimited possibilities within the organization. Most effective and instinctive leaders do this naturally and effortlessly. And if not, trust the better angels of your character and be prepared for surprising results.

SUMMARY

FOUNDATIONS OF LEADERSHIP
- Lead from a position of Service
- Genuinely Care About People
- Do the Right Thing is always the basis
- Believe People Always affect the organization
- Employee Impact is a valid pathway to Success

CORE BELIEFS
- It's amazing what can be accomplished when you don't care who gets the credit.
- Nothing is impossible when you don't have to do it.
- The authority vested in a Leadership role requires offering the invitation to contribute.

LEADERSHIP ASSETS (not all-inclusive)

VALUES	SKILLS	PASSION
Honesty	Communication	Confidence
Sincerity	Technical	Enthusiasm
Courage	Social	Accessibility
Compassion	Visionary	Empathy
Initiative	Sense of Humor	Visionary

Chapter 4:
The Culture

People are the heart of the culture. People are powerful, passionate, and endowed with magical capabilities. The culture of the organization is the accountability of the leadership. The leadership is accountable for creating and nurturing a culture that releases that power, passion and magic. Regardless of the scope of accountability or the size of the area, department, or facility, leadership must be the steward of "how we do things around here." Leadership is about many things, but at the core it carries the accountability for positive results. When leadership does not make an impact on the organization and produce results, something must change. In most cases, it's the leaders. As is commonly believed, "sometimes the only way to change the people is to change the people."

To assume ultimate accountability for an organization is to assume accountability of the actions, values, and performance of its people. To many this means power, control, and authority. Those are true elements of the leadership roles, but they cannot be the ultimate defining elements.

Those roles carry both a heavy burden and a huge impact potential when viewed from a different perspective. This new perspective is based on the role's ability to not only have an impact on the outcomes of the organization but the potential for positive and negative impact on the quality of life for everyone in the domain of the role.

From a position of service, with a genuine love of people, the role can effect change in people's lives and ultimately change the organization. This change, coupled with a well-defined vision, can drive improved performance and profitability. Positive results are the product of a positive, inclusive culture.

Common sense has always dictated that if people in the organization have passion for their work, are valued as contributors, and are well trained and well informed, the result will be positive. More importantly, this culture will regularly yield heroic gains as opposed to status quo performance.

The site leader holds one advantage: he or she can mandate the culture throughout the facility. Although a department leader can have an impact on his area, he is subject to the site leader's style and directives. Even so, the area leader can achieve great results within his area of accountability, even if he cannot influence the larger site.

The culture in a facility or department makes an impact on its output. The product or process operates within a specific culture that defines "how we do things." It follows, as stated earlier, that the accountability for the culture lies with the leader. Webster's defines culture as "the set of shared attitudes, values, goals and practices that characterizes an institution or organization." This is the domain and accountability of the leader.

As we define the word "culture," we must, as leaders, define the organization's culture. Are the attitudes, values, and goals truly shared or are they just embedded in the vision or mission statements, handbooks or banners on the wall? Has leadership created an environment where they are evident in the behavior of the entire organization? Again, the employees, as a group, cannot establish and nurture this environment. Leadership must first define, then create, then nurture and mandate the culture of the organization. A key word in the definition is "shared." Again, this implies an inclusive culture that cuts across roles and accountabilities.

Defining the culture begins with an understanding of four elements:
1. Understand what you have.
2. Define what you want.
3. Analyze the gap.
4. Ask, "How do we get there?"

Chapter 5:
The Culture You Have Now

<u>Understand what you have today.</u> This exercise is clear when starting a new business or building a Greenfield site. New employees, new processes, and new practices all represent a blank sheet. From day one, certain values, policies, processes and systems can be implemented that can define the culture of the organization. Each day you can build on those elements and with proper consistency and oversight, and reinforcement the culture will take hold and truly become "how we do things around here."

The "legacy" organization is different and in most cases, more difficult. The culture is established and has been embedded by years of events, perceptions, and behaviors. One characterization of those perceptions was the term "mythologies," meaning "what someone 'believes.'" This was introduced and taught by the organizational expert, Elliot Jacques, in his work on stratified systems theory. It is also referenced in the work of Ian McDonald, Catherine Burke, and Karl Stewart in their book, <u>Systems Leadership</u>, which explored the idea that what someone believes to be true is true, at least to them. That belief, real or perceived, becomes reality for that employee. Such mythology will only change when events or behavior convinces the employee that things are different.

Leaders can believe certain things, but they must understand how employees view those issues. So leaders must understand what they actually "have." It might not be what they think they have. Even if there is data, historical facts, and documentation, it might be perceived differently by the workforce. All leaders are guilty of getting bogged down with work. It can be easy to isolate yourself, convinced that the responsibilities of the role require you to hunker down and run the business. During those times we can easily misread the culture and the health of the organization.

The organizational culture will reflect different elements of the business. The primary focus or product of the business may have a heavy influence on the culture. Is the business a service organization? Sales? Manufacturing? Are the employees in a highly technical field, a mixture of skilled and unskilled labor, professional occupations, or highly educated or other specialized fields? Is your product a thing that can be used and touched, or is it ideas and expertise or a service? Although those factors don't predispose an organization to a certain culture, the nature of work and the workers will create certain sensitivities that can help shape the culture of the organization.

The world of a factory shift employee is much different than that of a sales customer service representative. A department of engineers operates in a working environment that is much different than the world of plumbers. This is a common-sense premise, but again, understanding the work environment is important for the purpose of changing the culture.

Management must recognize those differences not just in people but in their vocations. Although all employees of the organization will share the same mission, the same metrics of success, and the same objectives, they all approach their respective jobs differently, and most importantly, they view their roles differently.

Consider professional engineers. Those are technical and analytical personalities focused on a very prescriptive method of achieving objectives. Things operate in a certain way and things happen as a result of clear laws of physics and formulas.

They solve problems; invent things, fix things and make things work to achieve a specific objective.

Consider the professional sales executive. Aggressive, assertive, confident and extroverted, they talk, persuade, and sell. They identify needs—and, in some cases, create needs—for which they can provide the customer with a solution.

Consider the professional accountant. Analytical, methodical, and totally objective. The numbers don't lie. They keep the pulse of the business, deliver the economic news objectively and see the world in positive and negative variances.

We could go on with the various disciplines and employees of the organization. Again, management must pull all those types together into a culture that allows every component to function at its optimal level. This environment or culture of the organization is a critical component of success. Identify it, understand it, and shape it to the needs of your employees and your business and you will begin to create a competitive edge.

Understanding your current culture begins with examining a few revealing issues:

1. <u>What influence does my product or specific business have on the culture?</u> As discussed above, are there specific requirements of the business that dictate "how we do things around here?" For example, is there a process that may limit communication and employee interaction? Is it a heavily secured environment that requires significant monitoring and regimen? Is yours a creative business that requires an open, casual atmosphere that nurtures ego, creativity, and innovation? Many organizations will have a combination of those factors under one roof.

2. <u>Is there a legacy management style which has dominated the organization?</u> Is there a command and control culture that

holds decisions within a tight circle? Is it a consensus culture, in which many contribute to the solutions and processes? Is it just "the way it's always been done here?" There are libraries filled with works on management styles, pro and con, and the impact each have on the organization. Two common descriptions are the "authoritarian" and the "permissive." There is distinct science to both, and most experts will agree that both must be used effectively to drive success in any organization.

Obviously, the guiding fundamental of this book is the benefit of building an inclusive culture that harnesses the contributions of all employees. That would suggest that the cons of the authoritarian style far outweigh the benefits. My experience suggests that this style, although beneficial in some situations, if used extensively will severely limit the potential gains of the organization. The inclusive culture, which brings people into process-design, process-implementation, and problem-solving processes, will drive both incremental and heroic gains into the culture of the organization. This might be shown by the following illustration. (See illustration 1)

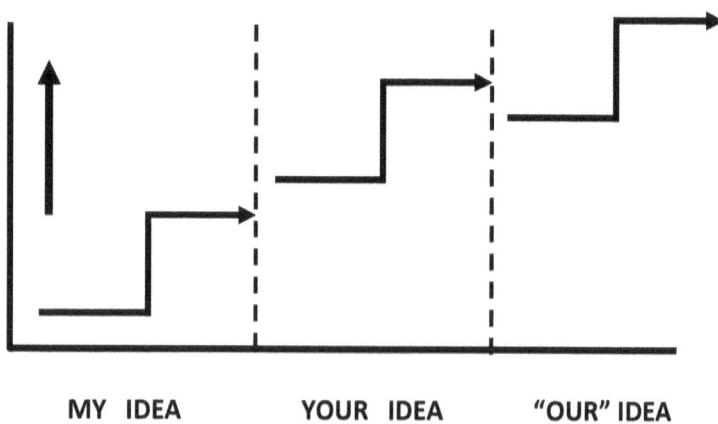

Although not a scientific or complex illustration, it suggests that we create our best opportunity for continued progress by incorporating all our resources in the work of improving the organization.

3. <u>How does the organization's current culture feel?</u> When you walk through the facility, how does it feel? When someone else walks through the facility, can they sense the culture? For example, can your customers get a sense of "how we do things around here" when they visit? What message do your employees send when visitors or corporate executives are in the facility?

Every culture, positive or negative, has a certain feel. Over my career, I've had the occasion to visit many manufacturing plants, large and small. In every one, I could sense the culture of the facility in a short time. It was evident in the employee's actions, their body language, their interaction or lack of it and, most telling, their openness in greeting and talking with visitors. It also shows in the housekeeping, workplace organization, safety and communication visuals, bulletin boards, etc. Without question, the most accurate barometer of the facility's culture is the employees and their demeanor.

The other significant indicator was the interaction between leadership and the employees during those visits. When the discussion is forced or staged, it is apparent. When the conversation and interaction is natural, comfortable, and genuine, you know it happens every day, not just when visitors are in the facility. Again, those are not academic or scientific findings, but they are the real deal. How does your current culture feel?

A natural dynamic takes place in any workplace. It can easily become about the work, the daily challenges, the politics, the relationships, and the results. Sometimes lost in the chaos is the customer. The focus can become internal, with the energy all directed toward the process. But the customer is always the objective. Without the customer, we have no business. As a facility leader, it was very rewarding when customers noticed and commented on the friendly, open employees. We worked hard at keeping our employees focused on the value of our customers. The repeat orders and long-term relationships were not accidents. We reminded employees daily that our customers were the reason we came to work. Although customer service, on-time delivery and consistent quality are the measurable elements of success, it's all pulled together when customers truly enjoy doing business with you, and it shows in your employees.

A culture that feels inclusive or feels good doesn't mean a culture without problems. The dynamics in any business are complex. It's important not to confuse "inclusive" with "problem free." One of the fundamental values of an inclusive culture is the consistency of values. Although there can never be 100% agreement, the common belief that the values are shared creates a platform for approaching problems and issues with a common belief that all are trying to do the right thing, both for the business and its employees. I can say without reservation, leaders and employees can feel those values in the organization.

4. <u>Is it working?</u> How does your organization measure success? Profits, ebidtda, ROCE, and sales dollars are measures of success for organizations. We can measure our human resource success by other standards, such as turnover, seniority, capabilities, titles, salaries, or other social standards. If the organization is not successful, actions are taken in order to turn the business around or

ensure that the business survives. In those cases, evaluating the culture may be low on the list.

Every business must continuously improve to survive and thrive. Continuous change is the norm in today's corporate culture. Programs such as Kaizen, lean, six sigma, SMED, and formal CI programs are practiced daily. Those can all have great value in improved capacity, lower cost, and higher quality, but the platform for all those process improvements is the organization's culture. It only makes sense to include the culture in the improvement evaluations and practices. If the culture is not engaging and inclusive of the employees, those process programs will fall short of the expectation and be difficult to sustain.

Chapter 6:
The Culture You Want

The next step in evaluating the organization's culture is defining what you want. Knowing what you have now can give you the direction for change, assuming you determine change is required. Many organizations have made definitive decisions to run their business in a certain way. They have opted for a culture that clearly prescribes the approach to the employees, the processes, and policies. The approach can be described in many ways, but for this discussion, we'll label it either inclusive or exclusive.

The inclusive culture is characterized by a leadership style that recognizes the value and potential impact of all employees. There is a level of engagement that allows people into the process of decision making and problem solving. This does not abdicate leadership accountability but adds dimension to the role. This culture involves a high level of frequent communication, both formal and informal. It involves the sharing of facility, business, financial, market and customer information. It has a high level of context of the business in the communication. It understands the value of having all employees know and understand what the business as a whole is trying to accomplish. This includes the union leadership, if the facility is unionized. To exclude union leadership is to invite division, rumor, and a fragmented message.

The inclusive culture involves all employees in improvement projects, including projects that originate from the ground up, not just leadership-driven or directed projects. It is an inclusive culture that capitalizes and optimizes the capabilities of all the organizations resources.

The exclusive culture is the opposite. It's characterized by a management style that plays it close to the vest. The domain of decision making is held by a few with the expectation that each role in the organization has very prescribed duties and scope. This culture is very cautious in sharing information as it believes most people are not able to handle certain financial or business information and will misinterpret the data. Ideas and projects are primarily leadership driven and of higher priority than those ideas or projects inspired from the non-leadership areas of the organization. This style generally regards unions and union leadership as detractors and can promote an us and them approach. Systems in this organization are designed and administered based on the belief that people will take advantage if allowed or will take the lower road whenever possible. This mentality operates in the belief that if a few rules are good, more would be better.

Those are two very distinct style of leadership that fuel very distinct cultures within an organization. Common sense dictates that most situations are not at either extreme and most organizations have some combination of the two. Businesses and facilities are dynamic, with people changing on a regular basis. Leadership changes occur in business on a frequent basis and the culture can be strained reacting to those changes. Most of the employees had seen a dozen general managers come and go over the years. The one constant was that they were still there and would be there when I was gone. It's critical for every leader to remember this important point. The question in every leader's mind should be, <u>What can I do to advance the culture and performance of this facility on my watch?</u>

Again, the choice will not be as black and white as described above. However, those are two distinct views of how an organization might look and feel. Understanding what your facility feels like today and defining what you want is the responsibility of every leader. It's as critical as effective cost control, safety, and quality control. Recognizing the value of influencing the facility's culture is a quality of the effective leader. At the end of the day, your facility will be stronger and maybe you won't have your name on the bathroom walls.

Defining the desired culture of the organization requires an examination of the objectives. The current state of the business is a good place to start. Every organization wants to be healthy, profitable and sustainable. Today's competitive environment in any business is challenging and dynamic. To stand still is to lose. Is the issue for change based on the survival of the organization or continued growth and competitive edge? Regardless of the objective, the time and effort spent on evaluating and defining the desired culture is time well spent.

While some might feel that organizational culture is just a touchy-feely element, I submit that it is the platform on which all the other business metrics operate. A typical list of business metrics might include:

Improved profits
Reduced turnover
Improved safety performance
Reduced costs
Improved customer service
Operational metrics improvement
Growth and acquisitions
Competitive edge
Talent retention

All of those have a common element. They are influenced by the performance of people. Most people don't live in a vacuum and are, to some degree, products of their environment. People have perceptions, develop beliefs, and have strong opinions about their quality of life, both personal and work. Until such time as our processes are fully computerized and automated, most businesses rely on people to do the work. If people are the core of the business and they influence performance of the business, then it follows that the environment they operate in is critical to the success of the business. This fact alone justifies the need to evaluate and define the proper culture for the organization.

The question for all leaders becomes, <u>what set of shared attitudes, values, goals, and practices will characterize the organization?</u> The next question becomes, <u>how do we get there?</u>

Chapter 7:
How Do We Get There?

The plan for culture change requires an analysis of the gap between what you have and what you want. If the core of any culture is the people, then the best place to start is an examination of the people of the organization. <u>If Leadership defines the culture, what leadership capabilities exist in the current structure?</u> Do the leadership qualities exist in the organization to affect the change required? If not, is there a sound succession plan with future leaders capable of making change? Any sustainable change must begin with the leadership of the organization. Leaders throughout the facility must be assured that upper management has mandated a change in "how we do things around here." Once that assurance is understood and confirmed, the real capabilities of the current leaders will be obvious.

This change must be driven from the top down with clear expectations to all facility leaders that we are going to do things differently. Assuming the defined culture change is in the direction of a more inclusive culture; Leadership must endorse and mandate an invitation to contribute. "As the leader goes, so goes the gang" is a real concept, and in culture change, it is critical.

If the current leaders possess the right communication, technical, social, and problem-solving skills, they can affect change quickly. Using those skills in a consistent, fair, and firm pattern will send the right message and begin to change how people feel about the organization. Leadership capability is the front line of culture change.

Cultural change must also include an examination of the capabilities of the employees as it relates to the specific business. This could include the education level, experience, and seniority of the workforce, and the complexity of the business processes. In some cases, the business may function with a high level of dependence on manual labor where the process is very repetitive and one dimensional. Culture in that business can and will play a key role in the feel of the business, but it may not be as critical as in a more complex business. Every business has informal leaders who can and will affect perceptions and performance. Effective leaders identify those individuals and use their status with the workforce to affect change and influence others. Have those individuals been identified? And how is management bringing them on board with the defined change? In this area, communication is critical in laying out the desired changes and insuring everyone at least understands the objectives and their role in creating the change. They may not all agree, but understanding the context and the purpose is critical.

The third area for analysis is the facility's legacy beliefs and history. Have there been a series of "flavor of the day" events leaving employees wondering what's next?

All businesses have a history of exciting new initiatives, all of which are designed to forever change the business. Each one is billed as the silver bullet and guaranteed to lower costs, increase output, improve quality, and differentiate us from the competition. Each is undertaken with the expectation of success. Most have not yielded the expected return and in many cases, it's difficult to remember when "we stopped doing that one."

Is there a history of not following through on projects or changes in the organization? If so, having a sound and reasonable plan for change will be critical. Making small, incremental, visible changes that will last is more important than making quick, superficial changes to the culture.

What is the history of management-labor relations? If the business is unionized, this relationship can shape how the workforce accepts changes and management directives. A well-planned series of discussions between management and the union leadership will be critical to affecting change. It will be important to have the union leadership involved in the cultural evaluation and defining exercises. This will provide the opportunity for ownership by the union and ensure a consistent message to the workforce. Even if the union leadership does not agree with or believe the management is sincere about a cultural change, management should still attempt the change. The consistent follow through by management will not be lost on the workforce, and acceptance will ultimately occur. Union leadership, as allies in the proposed changes, will make the process easier and timelier.

Some leaders in the organization have a lot of past "baggage," and most organizations and workforces have long memories. It's a convenient ploy for employees to bring up past mistakes and events when confronted with change. In some cases, the past transgressions are true and some instances are exaggerated with time. Every leader who has made decisions, disciplined employees or communicated unwanted changes has detractors. Again, the only way to counter those is to communicate honestly and demonstrate consistent values that reflect the new culture. People have to see change in order to believe change.

In this time of economic crisis where confidence in corporations is eroding as quickly as 401(K) s, it is critical to evaluate the culture of our businesses. Government bailouts, overhauling of financial institutions and stimulus spending may or may not fix the economy. It will be to the businesses and corporations of this country to look internally and, in many cases, redefine how they views their markets, products, services, and employees. As of this writing, the situation is unprecedented as American icons and blue chip companies are spiraling downward. As we re-tool our processes, products, and finances, let's also look closely at the culture in which we provide for our most important asset, our people.

SUMMARY
THE CULTURE

<u>Culture</u> – <u>The set of shared attitudes, values, goals, and practices that characterizes an institution or organization.</u>
<u>Shared implies an inclusive culture.</u>
<u>Management accountability</u> — <u>to define, create, nurture and mandate the culture of the organization or institution.</u>

<u>Defining the Culture</u>
1. Understand the culture you have.
    a. Influence of products or processes on the culture
    b. What is the legacy management style of the organization?
    c. How does the current culture feel?
    d. Is it working?

2. Define the culture you want.
    a. The inclusive culture
    b. The exclusive culture

3. How do we get there?
    a. Are the leadership qualities present in current management?
    b. What are the capabilities of the current workforce?

c. What are the facility's legacy beliefs, perceptions, and history?

The organization's culture is the platform on which all other business metrics operate.

Chapter 8:
The Manager and the Work

Webster's defines a leader as one who guides, shows the way, entices, influences; one who directs or governs. It defines a manager as one who administers, conducts and directs. All leaders are managers but not all managers are leaders.

For this discussion let's use the title "manager" for the individual with the accountability for the facility, the department, the shift, or the area. We'll assume this individual possesses the qualities of an effective leader and puts those qualities into practice.

Previously, the discussion outlined my views on the foundations of leadership and the values of defining and nurturing an inclusive culture in the organization. An effective leader, using good tools and operating in this environment, can create powerful outcomes. This discussion will attempt to outline some of the tools I found effective in not only managing the day-to-day scope of the business but also in optimizing the performance and understanding of the employees. This is especially important because typically, managers don't make or sell products — the employees do.

In my first role as a plant manager, I had accountability for a manufacturing plant with about 250 employees. This plant operated 24/7 with four shifts on a site with about 10 acres under roof. The production and maintenance employees were represented by national union with both a master and local contract. The plant had an annual budget of approximately $70 million dollars. It was a perfect size and structure for implementing and validating many of the cultural and leadership techniques I valued. Within about 50 paces from anywhere in the plant, you could touch a number of the employees through conversation, observation and interaction. The size of the workforce and the plant made it possible to get feedback instantly, and the plant could respond quickly to decisions, changes in direction, and processes.

This site provided an excellent opportunity to test and validate my beliefs about the power of an inclusive culture. The response was very positive and the plant performance reflected the inclusive culture we were attempting to develop. After four and a half years, I was transferred, leaving the plant with higher capacity, lower operating costs, improved safety, improved quality, and a positive outlook on the future, thanks to the skill, experience, and dedication of the incredible people in this Ohio plant.

However, when I first arrived, I found a culture far different than the one we would eventually define. One of the most glaring aspects of the culture was the situation I discovered with the parking lot. The plant had two parking areas divided by a guard house and a chain link fence. Both lots were used and generally full so I interpreted this as a first-come, first serve situation. Upon investigation, I found that the hourly union employees all parked in the outer lot and passed through the guard house at the beginning and end of their shift. The salaried employees all parked in the inner lot closest to the building and drove past the guard house as they came and left work each day.

In discussions with the department managers, I discovered this arrangement was made some years earlier after there had been a series of thefts in the plant. Curiously, the solution to the thefts was to require all hourly employees to pass through the guard house so lunchboxes and satchels could be searched. The salaried employees would continue to park inside the fence and could enter or leave the plant directly from their vehicles.

Without realizing or intending to do so, the management had sent a strong message: If you were hourly, you might be a thief, and if you were salaried, you were not. The message cut deep and generated mistrust, resentment, and anger. It was a dramatic symbol of the culture and the perception of "us vs. them." That, combined with the covered parking spot reserved for the plant manager, provided a great opportunity to redefine the culture and begin changing perceptions. We immediately revoked the parking assignments, connected the two parking lots and removed the reserved covered shelter for the plant manager. Parking became an equal-opportunity event. It was a good start. The reaction was instant, positive and represented real change in "how we do things around here." However, for some salaried employees, the reaction was not quite so positive, and for a while, they expressed their discomfort with the decision by moving their cars to the outer lot. That reaction surprised me, but soon they too began to see positive cultural changes in other areas and the parking lot issue was put behind us.

The parking lot was just one of several systems that enabled and hardened the dividing lines and perceptions between salaried and hourly employees. By changing those systems and creating a culture in which fairness, transparency, and communication were not only the norm but expected, the plant was positioned for greater productivity, creativity, and profitability.

My next assignment was as the general manager of a much larger and more complex manufacturing plant. This facility employed 850 people on a 1300-acre site, 45 acres of which were under one roof. The annual budget was around $160 million dollars, which supported multi-faceted processes including casting, rolling, finishing, coating and all the support functions required to produce over 2500 different SKUs, or product specifications.

Although I was confident in assuming this role, assuming the accountability for a large complex facility is a daunting proposition. When I reflected on the responsibility, I was confident, but I was also humbled by the fact that the success of the facility and the quality of life for 850 families were now my accountability. As I did in my previous general manger role, I took this responsibility very seriously.

In this role, I began to build on the models and tools I'd been developing since my first days in leadership roles. The physical plant was huge, the scope of the processes was wide, the labor relations history was complex and inconsistent, and the legacy issues were enormous, given the plant's 40 year history.

Chapter 9:
The "mSt" Model

How do you eat an elephant? With this cliché in mind, I began to think through a system in which I could categorize all the issues and the accountabilities that might confront me as the general manger. If I could mentally and literally group each issue, I would have a fighting chance at managing those many complex issues in a facility of this size. This is the basis of the "mSt" model I used to organize my thought processes: assess issues, assign the tasks, and solve problems. The basis of the model is that a people-centered culture is the foundation of "how we do things around here." It is the platform for the operating metrics by which we measure success. Operating on that platform are the mechanical, social, and technical issues of the facility. Every issue confronted in the plant will fall into one of those three categories. This was the first step in organizing the work of my role, the role of all managers, and the work of the employees. This was the first bite in eating the elephant.

The mechanical, social, and technical components of the model have both literal and figurative elements. While mechanical may refer to actual equipment and its operation and maintenance, it may also refer to those parts of the organization that are physical in nature, the hardware of the process. Technical may refer to those areas of knowledge and skill, the written documentation of processes and assets. Social, of course, is everything else, especially those areas that have an impact on the people of the organization. Again, following this line of reasoning, one can sort issues that confront the manager on a daily basis. Although the sorting doesn't solve problems or identify issues, the sorting points us to the specific systems or processes in place that apply to those various elements of our business. The following illustration shows the basis for the "mSt" model. (See illustration 2)

"mSt" Model

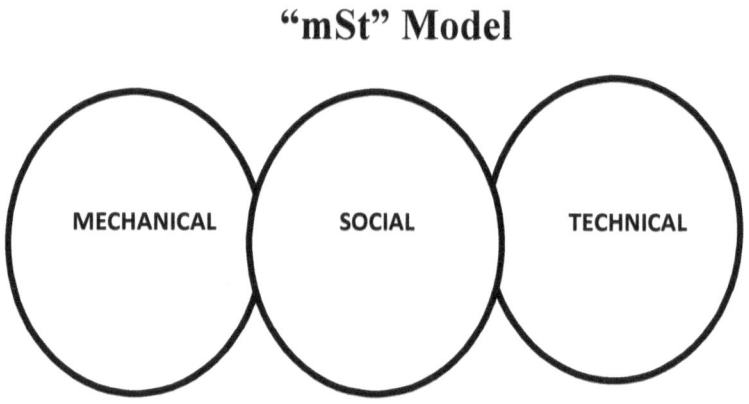

A People-centered culture is the Foundation

Chapter 10:
m — The Mechanical Element

The mechanical can be stratified into further categories that help the manager choose the best system or process best suited to the issue. This list is not all inclusive, but I used the following categories to describe this component:

>Equipment   Maintenance
>Property   Reliability

Equipment and property include the physical assets of the business. Regardless of the function of the business, there will always be some physical property. This property will have a cost, will be used or operated by people and will be subject to repair or replacement. Those three comprise a formula guaranteed to create issues for any business or any manager.

Equipment and Property

In my experience, this included all types of heavy manufacturing equipment and tools, ranging from a pair of pliers to 7000-horsepower motors driving a hot line reversing mill that reduced 26" aluminum ingots down to paper thin sheets. Obviously, this type equipment required significant electrical and mechanical maintenance, annual outages, and continuous parts replacement. The aluminum rolling mill, like many heavy industrial plants, has a wide variety of large and complex metal-working equipment, and it becomes the heartbeat of the facility. Uptime, downtime, reliability, throughput, units per hour, maintenance cost per hour, etc. — the issues are endless. Of course, each of those elements required highly developed systems dedicated to optimizing the reliability, output, and cost effectiveness of the equipment.

The plant property consisted of 1300 acres with 45 under one roof. The facility was 40 years old and presented significant infrastructure challenges. Water lines, gas lines, and electric cables required constant upgrading, repair or replacement. The annual budget and work load to repair and maintain 45 acres of concrete, lighting, roofing, and environmental controls occupied an entire section of the maintenance and engineering group. Whether to relegate the limited capital to maintaining the infrastructure or investing in new technology was a constant dilemma.

Maintenance

The cost to maintain equipment and property has a significant impact on the business. Just as regular and proper maintenance of your car is critical, so it is with the assets of the business. This can also represent tough decisions when faced with required output and tight production schedules. Shutting down for routine maintenance can sometimes be secondary to production demands. A clear understanding and knowledge of the equipment history, capabilities, and cost is critical to those decisions. The standing rule of thumb is to always take time to do the necessary maintenance, but there will be cases where postponing maintenance for continued production is necessary. Some scenarios will also justify a run-to-failure decision. In those situations, the manager must make very specific risk analysis decisions requiring a well-rounded understanding of the issues affecting the customer, the equipment, and the facility. In making those decisions the manager must also consider the impact on future production schedules and machine efficiencies.

The maintenance systems can also have an impact on organizational structure. Does the facility organize in a centralized or decentralized maintenance program? Most large industrial manufacturing plants have operated both ways over the course of their history.

A centralized structure will generally have all maintenance personnel reporting to a maintenance manager. The system will have maintenance supervisors, superintendents, and possibly planners reporting to the maintenance management group. This system relies on good communication between the production managers and the maintenance manager to ensure prioritization of the work and coordination of schedules.

When poor leadership occupies those roles or the general manager role, this system can result in confusion and unclear priorities. More time can be spent arguing or analyzing than actually getting things accomplished. The communications, systems, and relationships must be managed at all levels of leadership. If the production supervisor and the maintenance supervisor cannot agree on priorities and action at 2 a.m. on a Saturday, the facility and the customer have a problem. This goes back to the discussion about the inclusive culture with all employees understanding the vision and values of the organization. With clear guidelines and communication, leaders at all levels of the organization can make joint decisions that are best for the business.

Imagine the exclusive culture of command and control, in which only top managers have the authority to make most of the decisions. Line managers reflecting this same approach with their staff will see this reflected in the decisions of shift supervisors. Consider the following scenario: At 2 a.m., a machine has a problem. The maintenance supervisor wants the equipment shut down for repairs but the production supervisor has critical production quotas to meet. Neither feels comfortable in the current culture to risk making the wrong decision. Who wins — the production supervisor or the maintenance supervisor? One very common outcome has the machine down for a significant time while the two supervisors debate the right decision and ultimately call the manager to get a decision. The production and maintenance crews both sit idly by waiting for someone to do something. The result is wasted time, wasted resources and wasted money. Those structural and accountability dysfunctions are not limited to manufacturing settings. They can occur in any business.

In the decentralized maintenance structure, each department manager will have accountability for both production and maintenance resources. This has the advantage of one person being ultimately responsible for the output of the department. If production "owns" the equipment or the process, the maintenance of the equipment becomes part of the departmental accountability and ownership. This also requires the manager to understand his stewardship of the company resources and optimize both output and maintenance of the equipment in his charge. This structure facilitates an opportunity for the department manager to define a clear mission to both production and maintenance craftsmen. With clear accountabilities and defined systems, the supervisors can make decisions in a timely and cost-effective way.

Both structures work and both can thrive in an inclusive culture that engages all the organization's resources, clearly defines the shared values and practices, and allows people to make decisions and take well-calculated risks. Personally, I find the decentralized structure more effective as it focuses accountability and process ownership.

Reliability

The final component of the mechanical element is reliability. This concept addresses reliability and predictability of the assets, the ability to produce the product when scheduled, produce to the desired performance, and optimize the cost per unit produced. RCM, or reliability centered maintenance, is the science of this. It allows the organization to predict performance, and therefore plan production, downtime, and repairs to minimize the impact on the business. Many organizations have trained reliability engineers dedicated to those systems and utilize the latest tools of this science. As in all aspects of the business, the ability to plan and execute the plan is a significant key to success.

The following illustration summarizes the mechanical element of the model. (See illustration 3)

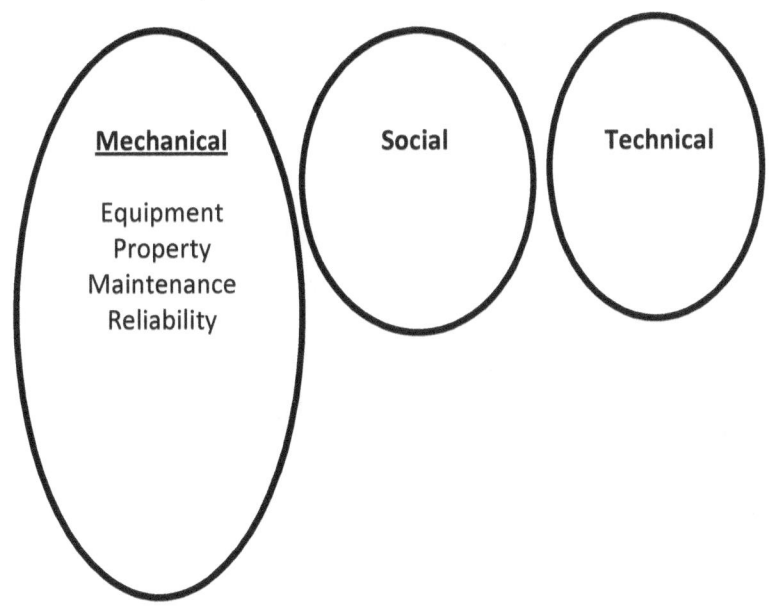

Chapter 11:
t — The Technical Element

If the mechanical element addresses the physical assets of the organization, the technical element addresses the intellectual assets, which might be defined as those documents and systems that define how the business operates. The technical element has the following components:

Training
Systems
Procedures
Policies

Those are broad categories, and each has many subsets. However, for the purpose of the model and its intended use, those capture the technical areas in most organizations. As stated previously, the model's intent is to provide a mental sorting tool to assist the manager as she deals with a wide scope of issues on a daily basis.

<u>Training</u>

Training is essential to any business, but many times it's overlooked or postponed due to the pressure of time and money. Forty hours of training per year per employee is a worthy goal but how many organizations actually achieve that objective. One area that particularly goes wanting is the area of management training. Managers are either promoted through the organization or recruited. Even assuming they come with the skills needed to manage, and many do, continued training in leadership is rare. The most neglected group is the supervisor. Many times those are the best operators or technicians, and we erroneously believe that their skills alone qualify them for leadership. They are placed in the role and left to their own best efforts to deal with conflict resolution, troubled employees, paperwork systems, substance abuse, and discipline.

Earlier in my career, I saw a supervisor training system that attempted to provide a variety of topics in a training format. The attempt had limited success because of what I considered a fatal flaw. The supervisors were taken off site for a three day session that had multiple training topics. The difficulty for the supervisor was the time away from the crew and the process. They often returned to administrative and process chaos that required extra effort and time to rectify. Many times the training was interrupted with phone calls from the plant. It was just too difficult to stay focused for that long.

When I assumed the GM role, we adopted a more workable and effective system. We first surveyed all the supervisors and asked them to rank, in order of importance, which topics they felt would be most valuable to them in their current role. We had some 20 topics, including recognizing and dealing with substance abuse, oral and written communication, union contract interpretation, plant-level finance, and confrontation skills. We then picked the top 7 topics and organized a one hour per week curriculum. We utilized the local technical and business college instructors, local GRADD (regional development organizations), career center instructors and our facility management staff. The supervisors came to the HR training room once a rotation for one hour sessions and then were back on the job. This system was cost effective, the needs were focused, and it optimized the use of everyone's time. This system reflected our continuing efforts to define and nurture an inclusive culture in the facility.

Skills training for production and crafts trades require a more formal approach. From a safety perspective alone, this is critical. Effective operation of industrial equipment is not a common skill, and therefore, training systems must be designed to meet the needs of the business. This cost can easily be justified as it meets the moral and ethical obligation of the organization to its employees as well as enhances productivity, quality and customer satisfaction.

Systems

The second component of the technical element is systems. From payroll systems to food service systems, businesses run on systems. System design can be complex and will drive employee and organizational behavior. People react to the rules, processes and boundaries of the system.

If the system is user friendly, people will use it as designed. If the system is not, people will find loopholes and shortcuts, or they will ignore the system and find other ways to achieve the same results. Many times the business has unknowingly built those roadblocks into the system. Then we wonder why people will not follow the procedures as prescribed.

Webster's defines a system as a method, a plan or scheme; an assemblage of things forming a connected whole. McDonald, Burke, and Stewart define a system as "a framework which orders the flow of work, information, money, people, material, and equipment." This captures the intent of the system as it applies in most businesses and industry. At this point, I would advise any leader genuinely interested in the science of system design to refer to the book <u>Systems Leadership</u>, a comprehensive study of systems and their impact on behavior and organizational effectiveness, authored by the three above. It must be said as well that this work heavily influenced the Commonwealth Aluminum Corporation, my employer prior to the merger that formed Aleris.

I have personally met all three authors and have a high regard for their work, concepts and theories. I will not attempt to recreate their work in this book but will reference it as it relates to the systems design. Systems, their impact and effectiveness, fit well into the element of the technical component of the "mSt" model. It will serve the manager well to have a working understanding of how the organization's systems drive the behavior and impact of the employees. This is critical to the development and nurturing of an inclusive culture.

If a system truly orders the flow of work, information, money, people, material, and equipment, every aspect of the business is affected by that system. People will be affected by how effective those areas flow, and therefore, the organization can succeed or fail based on the design and implementation of the systems. This alone makes the understanding of this area of management critical to success.

In both review and design of the organization's systems, the following outline may be helpful. Again, this is a condensed summary of the more detailed examination in the book Systems Leadership:

A. System Owner – Who is accountable for the output?
B. Purpose Statement – Has the purpose of the system been defined and communicated?
C. Flow Chart – A visual of the current or required system. How does it flow?
D. System Description – Instructions on how the system works.

E. Authorities and Accountabilities – Who has what authority within the system?
F. Control and Audit – Does the system achieve the desired output and can it sustain that output over time?

In summary, as the manager builds the inclusive culture, it is critical to understand that the organization's systems will drive specific behavior from the employees. Positive, powerful change cannot occur without a clear understanding of those systems.

Procedures

If systems describe the flow of the work, procedures can be referred to as the instruction book. It's the documentation that describes "how we do things," how our processes actually work. In the past, many of our work processes were considered art, a special skill, and rightfully so. Today, with the importance of various quality certifications such as ISO, TS, QS, the importance of repeatability and reduction of variances is critical. So much of our quality improvement work is focused on transforming the process from an art to a science. The science reduces the variation, which ensures the product is the same every time, every shipment, every purchase. Hamburgers from McDonald's in Kentucky taste the same as hamburgers in a McDonald's in California.

The adage of "say what you do, and do what you say" is the essence of those quality certification systems. And the heart of those certifications is the documentation or work instructions and how they are tracked, monitored, communicated, and utilized in the organization.

From the manager's perspective, in the problem identification and solving process, a review of the process procedures can be a good start. Are the procedures clear and easily understood by all involved? Are they well communicated and within easy reference and accessible? Are all employees following the procedures as written, or have shortcuts and bypasses crept into the process over time?

A common critical mistake in creating the procedures or work instructions is including too much detail. Things that sound good and look good on paper but don't actually happen in the process should not be included. Only include what you actually do in the process. Debate and decide what needs to be done and include those in the procedures, but only if they're actually done regularly. If not, take it out of the written procedures. Again, say what you do, and do what you say.

Policies

The policies of the organization become the final component of the technical element. Those documents describe the governing rules and practices of the business, including the behavior of the employees. They will define the culture of the organization as they include areas of impact to the employees. From the vacation policy to the dress code, employees will view the culture of the organization through the policies.

I can recall large policy manuals that resided primarily in the Human Resources department. I did keep one on my office shelf, but I must confess, I didn't refer to it except on specific occasions when an issue required a reference to the legalese of the policy. The point here is that those documents didn't figure into the daily management and leadership of the organization. They are generally known and understood, but do not become the driving leadership tool in nurturing the culture on a daily basis. The policies should reflect and be consistent with the leadership style.

In summary, the technical element of the model reflects the documentation and intellectual components of the organization. In the context of the "mSt" model, the manager can view issues through this filter and base decisions on the review of the training, systems, procedures and policy issues that have an impact on the organization's work and processes.

The following illustration summarizes the technical element of the model: (see illustration 4)

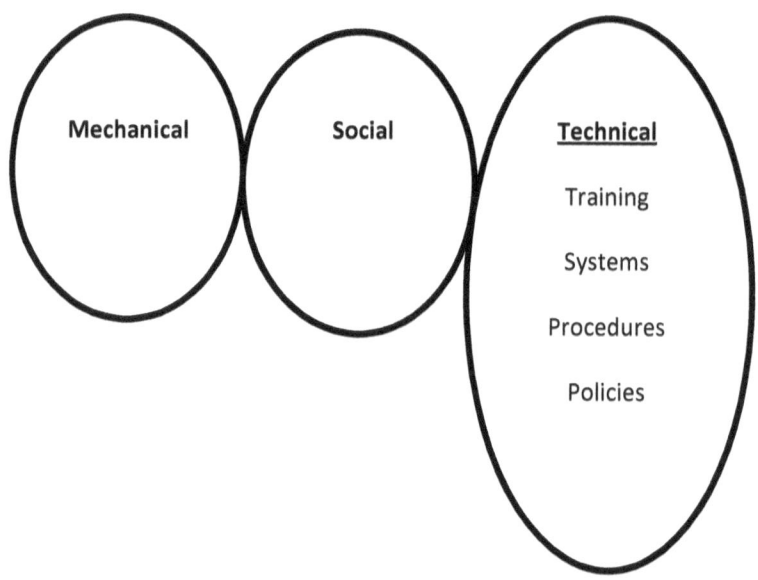

Chapter 12:
S - The Social Element

The mechanical and technical elements of the model are anchored by the social element. They occur within the social context of the organization and form the social platform. The premise is simple: all things mechanical and technical in the organization are operated by, supervised by, and managed by people. People exist in a social environment and management must lead the organization from that context. As stated earlier, management can mandate performance, behavior, and results, but without the understanding of the social dynamic, those become only papers on a bulletin board.

The components of the social element of the model might be composed of

People
Safety
Culture
Organization

People *are* the organization. This is the most important part of the business for the manager. Leadership is about creating a vision and bringing all the resources together for a common purpose. Assembling the right people with the right skills can address the mechanical and the technical components of the business. Defining and nurturing the right culture will allow the people to optimize their impact on the business. Getting the right people on the bus and in the right seats will allow the organization to optimize its competitive advantage. Doing this in a safe, caring environment will ensure the organization's moral responsibility to its employees and optimize their impact on the profitability and success of the business.

People and Culture

The earlier chapters of this book discussed the benefits of the inclusive culture and the impact people have on the organization. This is the centerpiece of the model, and as the manager develops this type of culture, its value and contribution will be obvious.

Safety

Here, management has one of its most significant responsibilities. Providing a workplace where the employees can work safely and with assurance is not only a moral responsibility but a cost effectiveness issue. A culture that assures employees that management is more concerned with employee safety than productivity is important to achieving optimal performance. Accidents and time away from work cost employers billions of dollars every year. The costs relating to accident insurance or self-insurance in medical bills, surgeries, rehabilitation are only a portion of the total cost of injury. Overtime to fill vacancies adds to this cost and can stress the employees covering those vacancies.

Safety awareness, proper training, proper personal-protective equipment, and well-engineered equipment and processes all contribute to the safe workplace. Incident investigation and root-cause analysis also help prevent accidents from reoccurring, and all of those should be part of the well-developed and implemented safety program.

Environmental compliance and monitoring should also be included in this section of the model. Today, health, safety and environmental (HS&E) fall under the same management, so those go hand in hand in the business organizational structure. The environmental compliance issues not only are critical to employee safety but also can have significant impact on the surrounding community.

Organization

The organizational structure can also fall into the social element. When you develop the culture of the organization, the structure will play an important role in the effectiveness of the business as well as the inter-relationships of supervisors, subordinates and support personnel. As mentioned earlier, it is not only important to have the right people in place, but also have the right people in the right roles. Having a clear vision of authority and accountability is critical to the proper communication of the organization's mission and objectives. A structure that isolates departments or segments of the processes can result in silos that break down communication and create territorial boundaries. Those can result in independent goals and departmental objectives that undermine the value and effectiveness of the business as a whole. It is counterproductive for one part of the process to be successful at the expense of the whole.

Proper organizational structure and reporting channels will prevent this fracturing of business success.

The following illustration summarizes the final element of the mSt model: (see illustration 5)

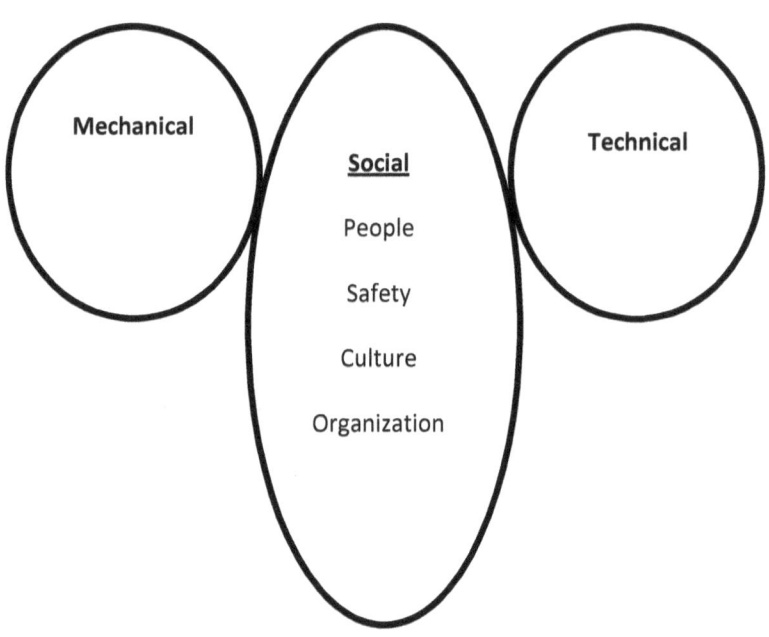

SUMMARY
The "mSt" Model

- A model based on an <u>inclusive, people centered culture</u> that sorts the issues confronted by every manager.
- Elements of the model become the basis for decisions, problem resolution, and outcomes.
- The elements of the model all have cascading processes, systems or procedures that become the next step in issue resolution.
- The social element anchors every issue in the scope of the business or organization.
- Every issue a manager confronts can be categorized as <u>mechanical, technical, or social</u>.

(See illustration 6)

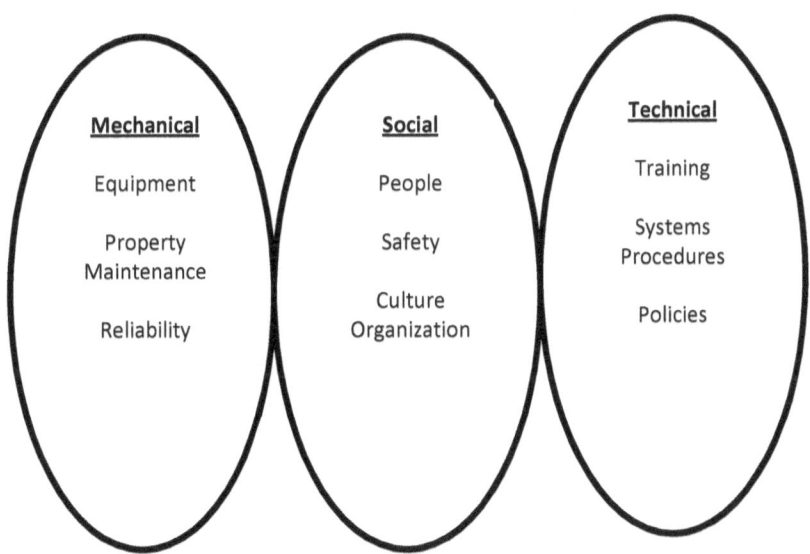

Chapter 13:
The Segments of Work (The Issue Map)

I believed obtaining results was dependent on effective communication and understanding. Making the communication simple as opposed to layered and complex was critical. Most people want to know why they are doing something, what they are trying to accomplish, and how to get there.

I saw a direct correlation between the level of engagement of people in projects and the effectiveness with which I or others explained the situation. Being able to create a word picture and get the "aha moment" from those doing the work was critical. Without it, even with the best intentions, people tend to flounder, hesitate, and stay confused. The beauty of this was that the communication didn't have to be overly technical, formatted, or formal. My best efforts were when I used the technique I called "squat and smoke." If you are from the south and over 50 years old, you probably know what I mean. If not, I'll give you the Tennessee version. Today you don't see many guys squatting, and of course, smoking is not popular or acceptable in many areas either. But years ago, especially in rural settings on farms, road departments, shops, and under shade trees in front of general stores, it was not unusual to see a couple of guys squatting on bended knee, having a smoke and discussing the issues of the day. It could be the weather, the local farm prices, or sports teams or politics. The subject didn't matter, but the gesture had great meaning. It was a gesture of trust. The gesture said <u>Time out; let's talk</u>. The gesture also indicated that anyplace could be used for this meeting of the minds. There was no set appointment or time to be at a certain place. There were no tables or chairs, and no room. Let's just squat under the nearest shade tree and talk it over.

The essence of this is very effective on a shop floor or in any business setting. Although you probably won't see people today in those settings squatting and smoking, you can see the impromptu conversations between managers and employees, either one on one or a small group, right there at the work station, machine, break room or desk. As an intentional method of communicating ideas, expectations, and needs, it can be very effective.

I often used the term with my staff as we discussed various issues and how best to communicate the importance of the issue. "Let's just squat and smoke with 'em and let 'em know what we need." Again, it implies trust, confidence, and honesty. Combine this with a simple, honest explanation of the situation and the need and you will get results. It also implies that the manager knows what she's talking about and has the ability to break issues down so they are understood. Remember, you are looking for the "aha moment," the recognition that what you are sending is being received.

With the "mSt" model, it's possible to begin to classify the many issues that a manager faces on a daily basis. This is consistent with the concept of simplifying the process of identifying the issue, finding a path to resolution and effectively communicating both the issue and the solution.

Another tool I've found useful in this process is the work segment model. It lays out a path for problem solving, improvement projects or anything that requires moving the business from point A to point B. The work segments or issue map are the What, Who, How and When.

The What identifies the issue, the problem, or the task, and it defines and communicates the context, purpose, and scope of the issue. It addresses the importance of people having a clear understanding of the issue or problem. People can function when just being told what to do, but why not give them the proper context in which the issue exists, the purpose for addressing the issue, and the scope of the issue? For example,

<u>What is the issue?</u> Our customer return rate is 20% higher than last year. This is causing our unit cost to go up by .05 per unit and we are losing credibility with our customers. This return rate is affecting 5 of our largest customers in our southern sales region.

<u>The Who</u> identifies the team that will be assigned to resolve the problem. It clearly identifies the leader and the team members with the appropriate skill sets best suited to successfully accomplish the task. It also identifies the support resources, either human, capital, internal or external. For example,

<u>Who is the team?</u> The team will be led by Joe, the South Region sales manager, with Sue, our top customer sales person, Bill, the plant production supervisor, and Betty, the plant shipping supervisor. Other sales and production resources will be available as needed, including representatives from our top three trucking companies. A travel budget will be available to accommodate customer visits, if needed. The team will have the main sales conference room available for scheduled meetings.

<u>The How</u> identifies the methods of approaching the issue, such as brainstorming, root-cause analysis, six sigma tools, continuous improvement programs, interviews, and other data collection processes. For example,

How will we proceed? The team will contact the customers, review the data on the returns, identify patterns or consistent issues, and proceed with the analysis of the data, identify possible causes, and test various solutions.

Finally, the When identifies the specific time line and deadline for the project. This can be hours, weeks, months or any time frame appropriate to the issue. This gives the team a clear end point to shoot for and identifies the urgency of the issue. This element, as with the others, can be renegotiated by the team as the work progresses and evolves. For example,

When is the deadline? With the impact on revenue and credibility issues with our customers, we must resolve this issue as quickly as possible. This project will be a priority for the team and we need a first report within 7 days. We should work toward an implemented solution within 30 days.

What, Who, How, and When — These frame the issue, the resources, the methods, and the time required to approach any issue and systematically work toward a solution or improvement. This tool provides a method that covers the key elements of any issue systematically. It can be very simple or very complex and layered with many of the scientific analytical tools available. Either way, it allows us to check the box and touch all the bases as we attempt to resolve issues.

The Work Segments or Issue Map might look like this: (see illustration 7)

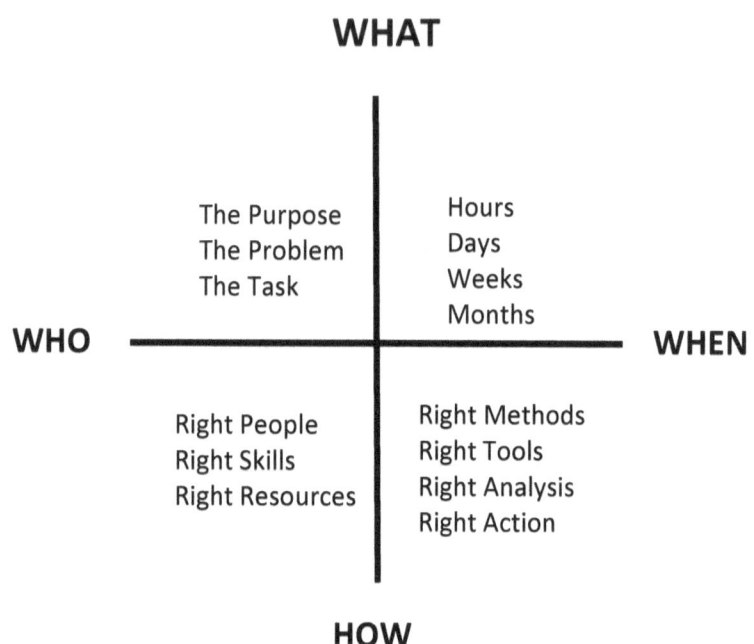

It's important to note that this model can be used both formally and informally. This can become a way of thinking when dealing with all types of issues. The thought process can be written out in a formal manner that clearly conveys the approach, but it can also be articulated in conversation or in a "squat and smoke" format. If the manager can internalize the model, it can be used to task work from the routine to the complex. By doing so, the manager is insuring employees have the best chance of success.

The model gives the employees the information, resources, and guidelines to successfully complete the tasks assigned. Again, this ensures that what is being sent is being received. Consider that most people are reluctant to ask for additional clarification on tasks. They fear appearing weak or less capable, so they listen, nod their head and off they go to begin the work assigned. If the tasking manager has done a poor job of articulating the true objective of the task, it puts the employees at a disadvantage and sets them up to fail. They may work very hard, expending valuable time, resources, and energy while thinking they are on the right track, only to find they fell short of the expectations due to a misunderstanding or miscommunication. Again, it sounds simple, but reality suggests misunderstandings are the norm, not the exception.

Use of the model provides the best opportunity for success. It is fundamental to the inclusive culture that engages all employees in the process. With the right information, the right resources, and a clear objective, employees, either individually or as a team, have the best chance of success.

Consider the above example on an increase in customer returns. Revenue is down, credibility is on the line with top customers and complaints are on the rise. This is an urgent situation that will affect future orders, profitability and the future of the business. Is this a customer-process issue, trucking or transportation issue, sales order entry issue or manufacturing issue? Could there be changes in the market that may be affecting inventories at the customer resulting in a changed customer specification requiring a reduction in inventories on previously committed orders? A variety of reasons may be at the root of this problem.

A typical response might be to first look at the manufacturing process, increase inspections, or shut down equipment for additional maintenance. If the response is predicated solely on the manager's beliefs or perceptions, there will undoubtedly be waste and undue effort that will not address the issue.

Using the model to get the right resources and employees involved and proceeding through the elements may not guarantee a correct result, but it will increase the opportunity to identify the root cause and work toward the most appropriate and effective corrective action. Once implemented, the fix can be long term, not just a lucky guess resulting in the problem reappearing later.

Another crucial benefit of this model is the ownership and engagement by the employees. Being part of a solution that has an impact on success and future security is important to every employee. "Check your brains at the gate and do what you're told" yields status quo indifference as well as resentment. Most employees want to be a valued part of the solution. It is the real competitive edge in today's workplace.

The model spans all aspects of business and industry. The application of the model can be used for issues including safety, social culture, organizational structure, production, maintenance, inventory, finances, and all-system processes.

This thought process can be useful in our personal lives as well. Personal finances, family issues and family decisions can benefit from this simple model of communication, analysis and action.

At this point, I want to reiterate the simplicity of the models and concepts discussed in the book. It starts with a genuine caring about the people of the organization and the realization that most employees want to contribute to the success of the business in a creative and passionate way. From this platform, the manager can begin to build an inclusive culture and consensus for success through a common shared vision. The "mSt" model is an excellent tool for identifying and sorting the numerous issues faced by managers in today's workplace. Issues can then be approached with the issue map model, which provides a clear method for analysis and corrective action identification. Again, operating from a platform of the inclusive culture, those tools can help deliver powerful outcomes in any business.

The next chapters will identify and discuss additional management tools that build upon the previous models and give the manager a program for day-to-day success that is manageable, effective, and builds powerful relationships that exceed the status quo boundaries of performance.

Chapter 14:
The Manager Tools

Libraries are filled with leadership books detailing a variety of management tools and styles. The manager's effectiveness will depend on many skills, including style, organizational and time management, analytical, decision making, and communication skills, among other things. The following discussion will deal with the tools I found effective in communicating the objectives, metrics, and vision of our organization. Those deal primarily with communication tools but also have an impact on tasking, monitoring, and reviews as a method to ensure a common focus on our goals and objectives.

Those may be referred to as the "soft" management tools as opposed to the more "scientific" or "hard" tools such as Six Sigma, Continuous Improvement Programs, Root-Cause Analysis, etc. The soft tools include the 9:30 Meeting, Plant Communication Programs, Management Review, and a program I call the "bucket system." All those tools have been effective as enablers to communicate and drive continuous improvement in an inclusive culture.

Chapter 15:
The "9:30 Meeting"

The core of this meeting is that it happens daily as opposed to the normal manager's weekly staff meeting. It's most effective in the first part of the day, and 9:30 worked best in our specific situation. Another time, earlier or later, might be better for others.

In my early years as a department manager, we had regular weekly staff meetings with the general manager. Those were effective but usually lengthy and covered a large agenda. In a large facility, it was easy for departments to become isolated silos. The real estate was large enough and the workload heavy enough that the managers could virtually go for days without seeing each other or talking to each other. This perpetuated a territorial environment, with each manager focused on his or her area and specific objectives. It led to strategies or tactics which optimize the various processes while sub-optimizing the whole. A situation like this can occur easily in an intensely competitive environment. And of course, when large volumes of product are produced every day, letting a week go by without review and interaction can have devastating results in productivity and quality.

The daily 9:30 meeting addressed those issues and more. We chose 9:30 a.m. because our shifts began at 7 a.m. and each department manager had an 8 a.m. meeting with his staff. Those departmental meetings were usually standing meetings during which the department's issues over the last 24 hours were reviewed along with critical issues facing the next 24 hours. This allowed everyone to get settled in their day, and to understand the current status of the department and the day's priorities.

The 9:30 meeting was held in a conference room located in the production area of the plant. This sent a clear message that the priorities were the manufacturing processes. The meeting was officially facilitated by our Planning and Logistics Manager as he was accountable for the loading and scheduling of the plant. He also worked closely with Sales on all customer orders and had the best perspective on customer issues and priorities. Although it was his meeting, as the general manager I attended and helped facilitate the meeting. This allowed me to monitor issues, set priorities, and communicate changing objectives and critical issues. I also used the meeting to cascade information and objectives from upper management in Operations, Sales, and Finance. With this format, I could also quickly observe the morale and mood of the staff and crews. This was especially important in order to address issues before they grew into full-scale grievances and distractions.

It is important for the facility or department manager to attend the 9:30 meeting regularly and actively participate. Another benefit of this participation is everyone in leadership and critical support roles hears the same information and hears it from the lead manager. This reduces the risk of rumors or misinformation spreading across the facility. People are hungry for information, and if they don't get it, they will fill in the blanks. Rumors and speculation can do great harm in any size facility or any type of business.

The key participants include the process managers, the maintenance and engineering manager, their key superintendents and supervisors, the human resource manager, quality manager, finance manager or controller, and other support area managers. This gives the key leaders of the facility a 360-degree, 24-hour review and culture check. With this scope of attendance, every facet of the organization is educated regarding the latest issues, priorities, and needs of the business.

The basis of the agenda is the facility's daily production sheet or activity summary. Nearly every business uses some type of daily report. In our case, it was a single-page scorecard that listed, by department, the key metrics of the process. The sheet tracked the previous day's results and current status against the monthly goals. Safety, quality and other pertinent information, such as shipments, returns, and inventory were listed. Sales information was not included on our sheet as our sales function was at a different location.

The daily Operational Summary was the agenda sheet. We followed the process flow by department with each department superintendant and manager giving a brief report on his or her area. The report always started with safety and environmental issues, followed by production, maintenance, and quality status. Then any cultural or personnel issues were reported to the group. We followed the process through each department, then concluded with a once around the room for comments from support areas and other visitors to the meeting. As the general manager, I always concluded the meeting with any comments or communications relevant to the issues. The entire meeting would last from 15 minutes to an hour, depending on the issues.

If additional information was required on any issue, a side meeting with select individuals could be convened after the general meeting. This allowed a smaller group to dig deeper into issues as needed.

Traditional staff meetings were also utilized and convened on special occasions. Our daily meetings allowed us to deal with most issues. Anything that could not be sufficiently discussed and resolved, we continued in a separate meeting. The key benefit is the ability to react quickly to issues affecting the process and the facility in all key areas, social, mechanical, and technical. We could monitor the culture, deal with rumors and perceptions, and track key production metrics and customer issues in a timely and effective manner.

The meeting format gave us the ability to keep everyone on the same page and ensure that key leaders were interacting on a daily basis. Of the meeting's many objectives, one was especially critical. Every day we worked hard to find something to laugh about, a very important part of the inclusive culture. Business must be taken seriously since the processes are complex and the challenges daunting, but sharing a laugh every day helped keep things in perspective and brought people to a closer and more respectful relationship.

I believe this is one of the most effective management tools available. It addresses the key elements of communication, process review, corrective action, prioritization, and the sense of urgency needed in today's complex business environment. It is an excellent venue in which to demonstrate the leadership qualities and practices needed for success.

To illustrate the key points of the 9:30 meeting, we can use the Issue Map to lay out the process:

What – A daily Operational Summary meeting to review the facility's key processes, issues, and priorities and monitor facility culture and social issues.

Who – The general manager and key process managers along with leaders of all support areas, including Human Resources, Finance, Quality, Sales, Safety and Environmental and any corporate or external guests.

How – The meeting should utilize the facility's daily process review or scorecard as the primary agenda for monitoring key metrics and outputs of the facility.

When – The meeting should take place daily, preferably in the first two hours of the day.

Chapter 16:
Site Communication Meetings

The site communication meeting is a great format for reaching employees of the organization with a consistent, focused message. This tool builds on the inclusive culture and reinforces the sharing of important information on the "state of the business." It enables the facility leader to address current issues and objectives, future goals and strategies, and answer direct questions from the employees.

The effectiveness of this event is dependent on honest, simple and understandable communication. A common mistake is to wrongfully believe employees want to see complex graphs, charts, and data. Those events need to be more conversational, and the manager should always look for the "aha moment" in the faces of the employees.

The size of the organization and process requirements should be considered when planning the frequency and schedule of the site communication meetings. If the meetings are too frequent, the message is diluted and valuable production time is wasted. If they're too infrequent, you lose the benefits of real-time communication and risk letting perception, rumor, and speculation drive the daily culture of the business.

A quarterly schedule works well with most organizations. This allows for manageable reviews of key metrics, goals, cultural issues and calendar events.

When a cadence of those meetings has been established, the manager can also use site-update letters, postings, or a newsletter to supplement timely communication. However, the memo or newsletter should never be substituted for the face-to-face meeting on a regular basis.

There are three key elements of the site communication meeting: tone, content, and a Q an A session. Those areas can be covered in about an hour and will serve both the manager and the employees in building the needed momentum for the organization's success.

The tone sets the stage and the feel of the meeting. The first few minutes will determine your connection with the employees. By tone, I'm suggesting your baseline must be a positive perspective on the information. This doesn't mean you should sugar coat or delete important facts, but it does means you should approach the data, issues, and challenges with a positive perspective. Those sessions can easily turn into gloom-and-doom sessions or finger-pointing and blame-game meetings. The employees will pick up on this quickly, become defensive, and the potential for improvement or change will be lost. Honest evaluation of the issues and the challenges is critical, but it must be communicated in a positive manner.

When all employees believe they can make a difference and are valued as problem solvers, powerful outcomes can and do result. People can accept bad news and rise to the occasion when given factual information in a sincere, respectful way. When approached with the realities of challenges and expectations, people will respond if they feel they are a valued part of the solution.

The content is important in both the scope of the information and the format. The message may be the same in both the boardroom and the facility, but the format must be different. Obviously, this will depend on the type of business and the workforce. In a professional office workforce, this may not be as important as in a manufacturing facility where the workforce has not been exposed to more sophisticated data-analysis tools. As always, the speaker must know his or her audience.

A good starting point is a review of the key metrics and goals of the organization. Everyone wants to know where they stand. A "state of the plant" format is always beneficial and brings everyone up to speed on the current status of the business. The audience will dictate the most effective graphics, charts, or tables to use in this section of the communication. Here it is helpful to use a consistent format from meeting to meeting to provide consistency and familiarity with the material. For example, if you used a table to communicate the last quarter's productivity, continue to use the table at each meeting with the updated information.

After key metrics and goal updates, include a review of strategies, projects, changes, and other issues that are important to the employees. A good rule of thumb here is to err on the side of providing more information rather than less. If I believed there were controversial issues brewing in the facility, I included them in this section. This, in many cases, will dilute the speculation and the potential unrest that may be associated with the issues. My view was to tell them about it before they could ask me about it. While not making the issue easier to discuss, it instilled trust and was viewed as honest and courageous leadership. This was another way to build on the desired culture within the facility.

The next section would deal with any upcoming calendar events for the facility. This was a good opportunity to give notice concerning upcoming projects, customer visits, training, benefits changes, events, etc.

<u>The final section of the meeting was devoted to the question and answer session.</u> This can be a difficult time for the manager but can also be the most effective. Our workforce was not shy

and asked tough questions about matters that affected them, their families and coworkers.

I tried to cover most issues in the earlier parts of the meetings. This was effective in that I had already answered most of their issues before the Q&A session. This is another area where the 9:30 meeting was useful. Most issues that concerned employees or were controversial in nature would come up in the daily reviews. The 9:30 meeting often provided valuable information as I prepared the content of the quarterly communication meetings.

The critical point in this section is total honesty as employees always find out if the leadership has not been forthright or honest in their communications. Dishonesty will destroy trust, and as we know, once lost, trust is difficult, if not impossible, to regain. Common sense dictates the manager cannot tell all they know about situations, and every manager must make decisions regarding discretion. Some information is not for all employees' knowledge and certain customer or financial information must remain proprietary. Also, any information that can be misunderstood or not interpreted correctly might complicate situations. Some information should only be shared after careful consideration and discussion with the appropriate executives. Every manager must make those discretionary decisions. An honest and sincere "I don't know" is always acceptable in those instances where the manager has not had the opportunity to review the issue.

Honest disclosure of information relevant to all employees in this site-wide format will be a positive tool for productive communication and culture reinforcement.

Chapter 17:
The Visual Site

A picture is worth a thousand words. The Internet and cell phone technology has redefined how we communicate. YouTube communicates entire concepts in 3minute sound bites. Pictures effectively communicate everything from road conditions to the products we purchase every day. Visuals also provide another meaningful way to communicate and include our employees.

The visual site can range from a welcome and information board at the entrance to more complex and numerous visuals throughout the facility. The type used is not as important as the fact that your site has meaningful, well-understood visuals located where employees can see and use them. Digital and electronic message boards are common today and the information can change as needed. They are expensive, but when viewed over the longer term, very cost effective. Sign boards done professionally are popular, and local sign makers can design and develop signs specific to your organization.

Another type of visual I used was developed by accident but was extremely effective in communicating key metric information to our employees. I called it the "bucket system." It evolved into an at a glance type communication that was unique to our facility, our process, and our employees. When I'd refer to certain issues to communicate, I'd suggest we "bucketize" the information.

The bucket system came about in a conversation with our planning manager concerning the quantity of orders the sales organization was placing on the plant. Conventional wisdom would suggest that the more orders a facility has, the better. That's true, but it's critical to understand the production capacity of the facility. If sales orders heavily outpace the production capacity, customer's orders can be late, and if they aren't scheduled into the proper lead-times, customer satisfaction can erode quickly. It also needs to be understood that on-time delivery was a key metric of the plant and a component of the employee gain-sharing incentive pay program. This made the issue of orders vs. capacity important to the employees on two fronts: the customer's satisfaction and the impact on the employees' monthly gain-sharing check. Matters concerning income and employee pay can get emotional very quickly, and any situation affecting income must be thoroughly understood and communicated just as quickly.

There were a couple of prevailing theories on capacity within our company. One strategy was to book all you can on the plant, and the plant's production would increase to meet the demand. This view was generally held by some past executives and although improved capacity is always the goal, simply booking the plant at higher levels would not always result in an increase in production. This approach often led to disappointed and angry customers.

The other theory, most strongly held by myself and the operations group, was to book the plant at demonstrated capacity, meet customer requirements and have formalized and dedicated projects for increasing capacity. Through well-defined projects with specific timelines, the plant could incrementally increase the production capacity and have good expectations that those increases would be sustainable.

Those two theories were constantly being tested, and in many cases, the book more theory would prevail and orders would be higher than capacity in the weekly lead-time "buckets." The result would be that each week's bookings would have carry over into the next lead-time week. The plant would then be in the hole before the production week started.

From a culture standpoint, this could appear to employees as a method to control the gain-sharing payout. Although it wasn't, some legacy issues involving gain-sharing manipulation that would sometimes resurface. Again, this was a rather difficult issue to explain from a plant loading perspective as the metric was the result of the pounds of orders for the designated week and the number of orders in the designated week. Those were all calculated in an appropriately complex math equation, complete with the carry-over numbers from the previous booking week, all divided by the pounds and orders available. Poof, you get the on-time delivery number and — what do you know? — It's bad again this week and the payout will be less. Better luck next week. You get the idea.

So in a casual, squat and smoke conversation with a group of employees regarding the idea of booking the plant heavier than our capacity, the "bucket" concept was born. It started with an aha moment when one of the group made the connection to the old familiar cliché of having ten gallons of stuff in a five-gallon bucket. The employee had successfully reduced the problem to a widely familiar and easily understood concept. From that day on, the issue was characterized by the weekly "order buckets." We completed the association with a large visual board in the main plant entrance that depicted the next five booking weeks as buckets on the board with the level of orders colored in each bucket. This comparison also helped illustrate and communicate the need to increase our capacity — the need to make our five-gallon bucket closer to the needed ten-gallon bucket.

The "buckets" soon became accepted conversation and it was amazing how the workforce picked up on the concept. What had been overly complex to most now was understood in the terms of what contribution they could make to increase the production capacity of the facility. Every aspect of productivity improvement was put in the context of increasing the size of the buckets so sales could take more orders. If Sales took more orders, the extra business would provide more job security both now and in the future. With more orders and more total productivity, there would be more gain-sharing dollars. The concept was effective on many levels and was part of the daily conversation.

Another use of the buckets and the "bucket board" came in 2003 when business fell off sharply for about 6 months. As business was declining, the employees could see it in the metal flow in the plant. The conversation quickly turned to potential layoffs and other cutbacks. In one of our communication meetings, we reminded everyone of the bucket board and the five weeks tracked on the board. By watching the board and seeing how far out the buckets were filled, the employees could get an immediate read on the business levels over the next 5 weeks. As I've said before, people can take bad news well if they get it in a timely and honest manner.

The bucket board didn't always have good news, but it was there every day when they came to work, and with just a glance, they had a good idea of what was ahead. It was during this time that we chose to reduce our cost through shift reductions, equipment shutdowns and other means as opposed to a layoff. Everyone kept their job and benefits and we still reduced our cost by several million dollars. The business levels rebounded in the fall and we were able to return to full schedules instantly, maintaining our safety, quality and productivity gains.

The bucket illustration and visuals fit our facility. I often challenged our staff to look for ways to bucketize other issues or concepts. The old KISS theory — keep it simple, stupid — still works. I challenge you to find a way to bucketize some of your business practices and concepts in order to foster quick, efficient understanding and communication of the key issues in your business.

Another way we changed thinking and communication of issues was with our quality. In our business, recycling is a major aspect of aluminum production. A significant cost saver in energy and material, recycling allows us to make use of the process scrap generated by re-melting the material.

We also use the melters in our cast houses to melt the scrap or rejected aluminum coils used during our production process. If a coil of aluminum is damaged or the quality is made unacceptable for any reason during the rolling process, the coil can be returned to the cast house where it is re-melted to molten and recast as a rolling ingot. At that point, the metal theoretically starts over and travels back through the plant. This can be a costly exercise, and great care is taken to reduce the internal rejections in our process and make it right the first time. This has obvious cost benefits and this key metric has an impact on not only unit cost but also on time of delivery, quality, and the plant's credibility.

When I arrived in 2001, the internal rejection rate of the plant was around 11%, which means for every 10 coils processed, just over 1 was rejected. That coil was sent back to the cast house, remelted to molten, re-cast as an ingot and rolled again through the process. For many reasons, it was critical to improve on this rejection rate.

The plant's product is aluminum coils. The ingots are cast, then rolled down to finish gauge, wrapped up in coil form and shipped to the customers. Throughout the plant, the work in process is large gray aluminum coils. With this environment, all the coils look the same and it can become easy to lose the value of each coil. The workers developed the attitude, "If this one is bad, just grab another one. They all look the same."

Part of the cultural change in how the employees viewed internal rejections was changing how they viewed the value of each coil. The coils, depending on where they were in the process, weighed from 17,000 to 25,000 lbs. The typical price of aluminum on any given day, in normal markets, is about a $1.00 per pound. This average price was real to the employees. With our plant located in a small rural Kentucky town, our parking lot was occupied by about 70% pickup trucks, so it became a natural fit to compare each big gray aluminum coil in the plant to a brand new F-150 Ford pickup. Without exception, our employees knew the value of a new F-150. Most, if not all, at one time or another, had kicked the tires on one at the local dealership. They knew the price tag ranged from $15,000 to $30,000 for a new one. The value of the coil equaled the value of a new truck.

My message was "For every coil we process, we take 1 new F-150 Pick-up and melt it down." That's the value of one coil when we reject it. That hit home. Every employee could visualize a new truck being dumped into the melter.

Our new visual was a board in the main entrance foyer of the plant. The board used small pictures of F-150s to illustrate how many coils or (trucks) we'd melted for the month. This was a significant factor in the reducing the number of internal rejections from an 11% rate to an average rate of 1.5% to 3% over a two-year period. Just as buckets became part of the language, F-150s became part of the plant language on quality. It worked and people understood the issue, understood their role in improving plant quality, and understood the impact of their improvements on the plant's future.

Chapter 18:
5S

There are a number of works on visual tools ranging from the electronic message boards to the 5S elements of the visual workplace. The key to all systems is the ability to communicate information in a timely and effective manner, not to mention the benefits of workplace organization, cleanliness, safety, cost effective inventory and the economies of effort.

No discussion of the visual tools would be complete without some study of 5S concepts as associated with Lean Manufacturing. This work is not intended to be a complete study of this concept but will hit a couple of the fundamentals. For reference and a more detailed dive into the 5S models, I recommend the excellent work of Hiroyuki Hirano: 5 Pillars of the Visual Workplace: The Sourcebook for 5S Implementation.

This work covers in full detail the benefits, fundamentals and concepts. Here's a quick scan of the elements as described by Hirano:

1. Organization (seiri)
   Organization means clearly distinguishing between what is needed and to be kept, and what is unneeded and to be discarded.

2. Orderliness (seiton)
   Orderliness means organizing the way needed things are kept so that anyone can find and use them easily.

3. Cleanliness (seiso)
   Cleanliness means sweeping floors and keeping things in order.

4. Standardized Cleanup (seiketsu)
   Standardized Cleanup means that Organization, Orderliness, and Cleanliness are being maintained.

5. Discipline (shitsuke)
   Discipline means always following specified and standardized procedures.

As with any improvement tools or projects, the approach is critical. The introduction and implementation of 5S must be carefully planned to avoid risk of indifference or a perception that it's simply the latest "flavor of the day."

Note that the 5S programs are not just for factories or production plants. This program can benefit any business and is applicable to all aspects of the business. Offices, plants, desks, stores, warehouses, and homes all benefit from the 5 areas of the 5S model.

Chapter 19:
The Visual Manager

The most important visual communication tool is the manager who gets out of the office, talks to employees and expresses genuine interest in people's work and their lives outside of the workplace. It's impossible to separate people from their lives outside of work. There's great value in developing an interactive relationship that allows people to learn about each other. This does not mean becoming friends with employees or allowing the supervisory relationship to break down. It means showing an authentic interest in what's important in people's lives. This builds trust and mutual respect, both of which are important ingredients for the cultural requirements of a competitive and successful organization.

Effective leaders do this in many ways. Some have daily routines that include walk-arounds at a specific time of day. Others have a more informal approach and let the issues of the day dictate their interaction. I also used the 9:30 meeting as a method of interacting with employees based on the location of the meeting. We held the meeting each day in a conference room located in the manufacturing plant. This meant a walk through the plant every day to attend the meeting. To and from the meeting there were many opportunities to visit with employees and discuss issues, both work related and personal.

The open door policy, the walk arounds, or a people person approach — it doesn't matter what you call it or how you describe it, the important thing is for the manager to be accessible and open. People want to follow someone they trust who is consistent, honest, and makes courageous decisions. You can build that trust more effectively by interacting with and taking a genuine interest in your employees.

Too often in those challenging times, managers are occupied with activities associated with managing the business. Conference calls, meetings with local and corporate staff, problem solving, and improvement strategies can occupy most of the day. It can easily consume the manager's time, and weeks can pass without meaningful interaction with employees. That's one reason the 9:30 meeting was important in my day as it forced me to get into the plant and interact with the people who made the metal.

Powerful outcomes will result from the manager who combines the technological and creative communication tools available. And powerful outcomes are, after all, the objective of our businesses and industries in this changing and competitive world.

Manager Tools

TOOLS	WHAT	WHO	HOW	WHEN
9:30 Meeting	Daily 360 degree summary of business issues	Site leader and all key staff	Central location to the process and daily activity sheet as agenda	Daily within 2 hours of start time in the a.m.
Site Communications Meeting	All employee "State of the Business" communication	Site leader	Open meeting with status and Q&A session at end	Quarterly or with appropriate frequency
Visual Site	Visual communication systems for at-a-glance key information	Site leader and key process leaders	"Bucket systems" signs, message boards, newsletters	Always with systems to ensure timely and relevant info
5S Program	System of Organization, Orderliness, Cleanliness, Standardized Cleanup, and Discipline	All employees	Identify start area and cascade through all departments	Ongoing
Visual Manager	Accessible and visible site leadership	All key leaders	Open Door and frequent, genuine interaction with employees	Ongoing

Chapter 20:
Management Review

If you want to improve something, you must measure it. If you measure it, it must be reviewed, analyzed and improved. Most businesses attempt every day to be successful and improve their sales, quality, productivity and profitability. Likewise, most businesses fail to succeed or adapt to change, not because of a lack of talented, devoted, and hard working employees, but because they fail to effectively document issues, identify opportunities for improvement, and develop sustainable corrective actions.

In our quest to improve our overall processes as well as documentation and records, our plant embarked on a strategy to become QS9000 certified. With the help of a very effective consultant expert, we started down a 2-year road to certification. We laid out the plan, which began with reviewing and documenting our work instructions. In other words, we attempted to write down what we did in minute detail. An important part of this exercise is to include the workforce as they are the ones who actually do the work. If not, support personnel will attempt to capture the process and will either build-in steps that don't actually occur or will miss the critical steps that have evolved over time within the process. So always include the people on the ground.

This part of the certification is the "say what you do and do what you say" section. (And only say what you really do. Avoid the temptation to be too technical and too detailed. If the employees don't actually do it, then don't say they do it.) We captured the work instructions of the processes, trained the employees on the expectations of the certification system, installed and implemented some new data-capturing systems and had our certification audit. At the risk of oversimplifying the process, we passed with flying colors and achieved our certification on our first attempt. We were thrilled and very proud of our facility and our employees. We now could fly the QS flag and proudly proclaim our certification to our customers and competitors.

This quality certification did something important for our facility: it required us to dramatically improve our documentation and review process. Again, we had good, hard-working people who knew the business, the processes and the equipment. We corrected issues every day and made improvements every day. What we <u>didn't</u> do well was write down what we did and how we fixed it. Our new certification system provided the tool to improve this part of our continuous improvement program.

About two years into our QS certification, our company entered the automotive market and we were required to upgrade our QS system to the TS certification system mandated by the auto industry. We did this with some ease and again, achieved this important certification on our first attempt.

One of the required elements of both those certifications is a documented management review process at least 2 times per year. This required a senior executive to be present and participate in a wall-to-wall review of the facility's quality program, opportunities for improvement, and corrective-action plans.

As part of our program to maintain the certification and successfully pass the required surveillance audits, we decided to go beyond the minimum requirement. We started a monthly management review process with the site leaders and invited a senior executive the required two times per year. We also developed a management review book that enabled us to standardize our monthly data and agenda. This book, over time, expanded to include a variety of support programs and schedules, including key financial, capital, project, outage, and inventory information. The book evolved into a user friendly everything you need to know about the facility handbook published on a monthly basis.

The book became both the agenda and the program for the monthly management review meeting we held with key departmental managers and support staff. The individual department's information was standardized where appropriate, and each area leader presented the data complete with key highlights, issues, projects, corrective action, and the forecast for the next month.

The value of this process was apparent on many levels. First, it provided a depository for the critical data of the facility in a standardized, retrievable, and user-friendly format. Second, it provided a forum in which the key leaders of the facility could interact and come to understand issues, accomplishments, and needs. Third, it gave me, as the general manager, the opportunity to review, challenge, prioritize, and provide context for the facility, our strategic goals, and updates on our business. Just as our daily 9:30 meeting provided this opportunity on a 24-hour basis, the management review process provided the same opportunity on a monthly basis. Everyone knew the issues, their role, where we were and where we were going.

The following discussion will outline how we developed the process. Again, using the Issue Map, we can lay out the process using the key elements of What, Who, How, and When:

<u>What</u> — Management review is a summary review process that details the key metrics of each area of the facility, its processes, and outputs. The process provides for a management

review book as a record of those key elements and a forum for detailed discussion, review, and analysis by key leaders and their designees. It provides a permanent record of data, opportunities for improvement and corrective action completed or planned. It provides documentation for improving business performance and contribution to profitability, ebitda, ROCE, and other business measurements of success.

Who — The process owner is the site leader accountable for the overall process. The site leader facilitates the monthly meeting, then recommends and approves changes in the content and format. The process champion is a key leader who typically leads the quality certification. This individual should also have intimate knowledge of the IT systems and data-collection tools as he will be accountable for compiling the area data and producing the final draft of the monthly book.

The process participants will include key area managers, their designees and all support areas such as Finance, Sales, Materials, Health, Safety and Environmental and Human Resources. The meeting should also include any productivity project leaders, Six Sigma Black Belts, or other key process leaders within the site. Outside guests should be included as appropriate and the key executives should be invited as necessary to meet any certification requirements.

How — The foundation of the process should be the quality certification system in place, such as QS-9000 or ISO-9001, etc. With those systems there will already be a data-collection system operating in the facility. If not, the key metrics of the processes should be identified and collected for analysis. IT support can assist in creating depositories and retrieval/inquiry programs to enable user-friendly tools. This data should be standardized as much as possible on area scorecards, dynamic documents that can be reviewed and revised as needed.

The data is compiled in a summary book and becomes the agenda and program for the monthly review meeting. A typical table of contents might look like this:

- Agenda sheet with participants
- Opening comments by site Leader
- Quality Systems Review (if the site has formal system)
- Safety/Environmental Review
- Finance and Cost Review
- Operations Review (Departmental Process Review)
- Six Sigma or Productivity Programs Review
- Technical/R&D New Product Review
- Human Resources Review
- Purchasing/Materials Review
- Sales and Customer Review
- Closing comments by site leader

Every business will have specific areas unique to their operation. The area manager or her designee leads the discussion in each segment, and the group participates with any questions. During this discussion, the site leader can probe the issues and recommend revisions to the content or reestablish priorities for review meeting.

The session should be given priority. It should be somewhat formal but not a recited presentation. It should be informal enough to encourage participation and discussion by all. It is critical to have a designated scribe to take copious notes to record minutes of the meeting for documentation. The book will contain information on the previous month. The December book will include the scorecards that cover the entire year.

The year-end book becomes a summary of the year and is an extremely valuable document containing key information on every segment of the business.

When — The meeting should be scheduled on a monthly basis. We found we could get the data compiled; the summary scorecards completed, and schedule the meeting by the 15th to 20th of the following month. The January review data would be discussed in the February meeting and so on.

The nature of the business can determine the frequency. Some organizations may feel a quarterly review is sufficient. Larger, more complex processes may require monthly reviews in order to keep the volume of data and issues manageable.

The meeting can range from two hours to all day, depending again on the nature of the organization. We found a monthly meeting that lasted from 2 to 4 hours was optimal for our operation.

In summary, this process is an excellent tool for review, analysis and documentation of the organization's key data, strategies, issues, and priorities. It provides a strong format for the site leader to further demonstrate strong leadership and a firm grasp of the issues. It also nurtures and strengthens the inclusive culture of the organization.

The process also sends a strong message to the corporate office and other segments of the business. It clearly shows a local sense of urgency and dedication to the business. It also indicates a local approach to the stewardship of the site assets, both physical and human.

This process should provide further evidence of the local management's pursuit of excellence and a culture of continuous improvement. It is a process that clearly provides an opportunity to combine the best of the mechanical, technical, and social elements of the culture to optimize the organization.

Chapter 21:
Building and Managing Labor Relations

There is stress in the workplace today. At this writing, the unemployment rate has ranged from 9.7% to 10.2%, the highest in the last twenty-five years. Legislation is pending that will make card check the law and install unions in workplaces where 50% plus 1 of the employees sign the card. The media and its commentary on corporate greed compounded by examples of CEO and Executive compensation excesses have broadened the belief that there is workplace injustice and disparity.

Non-union companies spend millions on "union-avoidance" strategies while unionized companies spend millions on grievance resolution and arbitrations. Each company must decide on its approach to its employees, regardless of its union status. Today's global competitive environment demands optimal performance of resources for survival and sustained profitability.

Whatever the union status, a people-centered and inclusive culture can direct the energy and experience of all resources toward optimal performance. It's been said often and accurately, "Management gets the union it deserves."

Management makes decisions that have an impact on salaried and non-union employees because it can, and it makes decisions that have an impact on unionized employees based on what it can successfully negotiate. One view of the union's purpose is to protect its members from unfair management practices and ensure job security. This has long been the basis of union solidarity and the foundation of the unions' agendas and programs. In this simplistic interpretation, it could also be said that unions hold a firm belief that management, if allowed, will opt for practices that do not protect the employees and, without the oversight, will ultimately widen the gap in compensation, benefits, and working conditions.

When both management and the union accept this premise, it becomes the natural line in the sand between the two groups. Too often this becomes the platform from which both groups base their approach and their behavior on the wide range of issues they face daily. The "us and them" mentality is the default starting point on every issue. It follows that the basis of that mentality is the absence of trust on the part of both groups.

The development and nurturing of an inclusive culture and the foundations of leadership proposed in this book speaks directly to those issues of trust and fairness. If the default position of management is to "do the right thing" and create an environment of trust and engagement, then it also follows that a new platform of working together can be achieved. This approach can greatly increase opportunities to resolve issues and optimize performance of employees and the organization.

The benefits of this approach apply for both non-union and union workplaces. If your organization is currently not organized, the inclusive culture is the best and most fundamental union-avoidance program available. This culture attacks the number one issue for unions: lack of trust in management. Likewise, if your organization is currently unionized, this approach can dramatically change the environment and the level of effective labor relations. The key is management's consistent attempt to "do the right thing," communicate and engage the union leadership in the resolution of issues as well as the strategy of the organization. This is not to be confused with conceding or sharing the accountability for the decision or the strategy. It suggests good up-front communication and engagement of the union leadership for context and purpose of the strategy and the planning of the organization.

Trust is a powerful element of any working relationship. It takes time to gain trust, and it can be lost quickly. Although management neither will nor is expected to get it right every time, the key is a high level of confidence that management, in every case, at least makes a genuine attempt to get it right and will always try to do the right thing. That level of confidence must start with the local site manager and the local union leader.

Chapter 22:
The Site Manager and the Local Union President

Trust begins at this level of the organization. An open-door relationship is critical in cultivating inclusiveness and trust. A demonstrated pattern or cadence of communication will break down past issues and begin to build the one-on-one relationship.

A different dynamic forms when two people have conversations instead of discussions. This will take time but it is important that time is invested in building this working relationship between the two leaders in the facility.

Although it is true that the employees work for the company and not the union, it is naïve for management to not acknowledge the allegiance members have to the union and its leadership. If nothing else, peer pressure and the group dynamic reinforces this allegiance. So if any true cultural change is to take place, it must start with the site leaders.

As the level of trust grows, the level and depth of communication can be used to educate the employees and the union on the broader business climate, company positions and challenges within the industry. Many times we limit our communication with the union to the local issues and what is good for the company, and many times this is interpreted as what is good for management.

Discussing the bigger picture begins to put local issues in context as they are viewed within the issues facing the industry and its specific markets. Local issues usually cascade from bigger issues and challenges faced by the company. Giving the local union leader a clear line of sight from industry and company challenges to the comparative local site issues is critical to their understanding of the local why and how. This allows the site leader to reinforce the company objectives for long-term survival and competitiveness. It also speaks to the most fundamental objective of the union: the long-term survival of the company.

Years ago I had a very enlightening conversation with an experienced and very skilled union leader. He shared a profound insight into the union and its members' four primary concerns: Survival of the company, assurance of the specific employee's job, assurance of wages and benefits, and a safe workplace. He also said, "Everything else is noise." I never forgot that conversation and I try to evaluate every issue within the context of those four concerns.

Survival of my company. If the company and the facility don't survive, then the other three concerns don't exist. So what is management doing to promote the company's growth and long-term success? What is management doing that threatens that survival? Given this context, it becomes critical as the site manager shares important information about the industry, the company, its strategies and goals. Enabling the local leader to understand the actions of management related to the company's position in the industry can prevent hours of second guessing and speculation about specific decisions or actions. Remember, I didn't say the local leader must be made to agree with management, only to understand. There is a difference.

Assurance of the employee's specific job. There is pride in ownership of specific skills. Most people want to be valued and contribute to a larger cause. Replacement of an employee with temporary or junior employees is more difficult when specific skills have been developed over a period of time. This addresses job security as well as job ownership. Pride of ownership and craftsmanship is in the organization's best interest. We can build flexibility and multi-skilled roles in our organization and still capture those benefits.

<u>Assurance of wages and benefits.</u> Everyone wants meaningful and value-added work. However, wages and benefits support our families and our dreams. This issue is easily the most inflammatory and emotional with both salaried and union employees. Recent stories of excessive CEO and executive pay and bonuses have intensified the emotion and met with a swift reaction. This gap in compensation further validates perceptions of greed and unfair play by those at the top of corporate America.

As business conditions deteriorate, the implication is that the rank and file will make the sacrifices to ensure the survival of the business. With the accelerated increases in health insurance, most companies are reducing benefits, increasing employee contributions to premiums, or both. In issues involving wages and benefits, serious, open, and honest discussions must take place with union leadership to ensure all parties at least understand the stakes.

<u>A safe workplace.</u> No one in management or the union wants employees to be at undue risk in the workplace. The reality is that many of our jobs are dangerous and the conditions imply risk. It is management's moral and legal obligation to do everything possible to minimize the risk to employees and provide proper personal protective equipment as well as safely engineered and guarded equipment. This is a perpetual process, and the work of improving safety in the workplace is never done. This position must be continuously reinforced with the union leadership, and the site manager must work to build that confidence and level of trust with the local union leadership.

When issues are viewed from this perspective, solutions and approaches to problem solving can be based not on emotion, but on realistic factors rooted in the honest attempt to do the right thing for the business and the employees.

The new culture must begin with the site manager. This is the fundamental idea behind the concept of leadership that claims, "The authority vested in a leadership role requires offering the invitation to contribute." If the site manager doesn't demonstrate a willingness to do things differently, it will not happen.

Without this invitation to contribute, the default position will prevail. The current culture, good or bad, will remain the platform on which management-labor relations are viewed. For too long in too many businesses, the default position has been that labor and management have different agendas and that fundamental differences can only be addressed through conflict and constant negotiation. If management truly has the accountability and the authority to determine the strategy and direction of the business, and I believe it does, then it holds true that management must make the decision and the invitation to change the way things are done.

This must start with the site manager as it relates to a facility or with the CEO if it relates to a corporate organization. This officially gives all members of management the authority to offer the invitation throughout the organization. There must be consistency across the organization in the approach to management-labor relations, and that starts at the top, whatever role that may be.

Chapter 23:
The Department Manager and the Committee Rep

Cascading the trust through the facility is critical. The site manager signals the change in approach, giving the departmental leaders the permission to follow suit. This drives the consistency of the information, objectives, and outcomes. The union's departmental representative is the central contact with the membership and the key to the message from management.

In most unions, the committee representatives are elected by the membership of that department. This individual is viewed as the formal leader of the area and will be the key to how the workforce interprets management strategies, ideas, and tactics.

Building a relationship of trust and open communication between the departmental manager and the committee rep is critical. A regular cadence of conversation and discussion is the primary tool to build and develop a trusting and effective working relationship between those two key leaders.

The frequency of meetings should be set according to the needs and size of the facility. At this level of the organization, I believe weekly meetings are the most effective. This keeps information current and allows the leaders to address issues at the early stages.

In the early stages of those weekly meetings, there will probably be a large agenda covering a variety of topics. This is especially true in organizations where this type communication with the union is new. Not being used to this accessibility to management, the union leader will bring every issue possible to the table. Some of this is the fear that the new level of openness won't last and that they must get all their issues on the table before the availability is lost.

As the cadence of meetings continues and trust is developed, the agendas will be more focused and relevant. The meetings and discussions will become shorter and more effective in identifying and addressing key issues in the department. Trust is an amazing enabler.

Trust will have an impact on efficiency. For example, after I assumed the GM role at one of our plants, I changed our stocking and distribution of office supplies. The current system was based on the potential for theft and used extensive controls.

Supplies — legal pads, pens, paper clips, etc. — were kept in a locked cabinet in the purchasing office. When someone needed supplies, he requested the items from the purchasing department staffer, who would then record the employee's name, the date, and the requested items on a notebook, then unlock the cabinet and hand the items to the employee. My first experience with this process involved a request for paper clips. To my surprise, the attendant handed me 5 paper clips after I filled out the required information.

In the plant's efforts to reduce and control costs, they had introduced a system that sent a strong message of mistrust. I immediately changed the process to a "kan-ban" system in which there was free choice of supplies managed by the vendor. The system required the vendor to restock the items weekly based on a min-max inventory. Initially, costs went and more supplies were used because the employees would get 3 legal pads instead of 1, 3 pens instead of 1, and so on until they trusted that the supplies would be there when they needed them. Costs fell once they realized there was no need to hoard supplies because the supplies they needed were always there. It also allowed the attendant to spend their time on more value-added work, thereby further reducing costs.

It works the same with relationships. If the opportunity to discuss issues and concerns is always there, the issues are relevant, the list is shorter, and valuable time is saved. That's human nature. Make the time available and it will pay huge dividends in building trust and efficient relationships, and that means productivity gains for the business.

The agenda should cover safety, quality and production data, social issues, departmental projects, discipline, grievance issues, and employee input. The important thing is to formally schedule a session with the departmental union leader. The scheduled appointment gives assurance there will be an opportunity for discussion. When the meeting time is left open and based on an informal, "give me a call or stop by when you can," more often than not the meeting never occurs. Set a time and keep your word. Then get on with the work of solving problems and changing the culture. Remember, it's amazing what can happen when you don't care who gets the credit. And remember that the authority vested in a leadership role requires offering the invitation to contribute. That's why you, as the department leader, must approach your rep, suggest the meeting, set the time, place, and agenda, and make a sincere and genuine attempt to begin the conversation. You will be building a new working relationship built on trust.

Chapter 24:
The Supervisor and the Shift Steward

The supervisor role in any organization is critical to affecting change and defining a culture. The supervisor is often caught between management and the workforce and is forced to choose. The choices, viewed from the supervisor's perspective, can be a matter of survival.

This is the leader closest to the people who operate the process and produce the product. Supervisors live on the front lines where the workplace environment can be the difference between heroic gains and status quo productivity. This is the level in the organization where the inclusive culture becomes real and its value is translated into a competitive edge in productivity, quality, and cost efficiency.

This is also the level of the organization where the perception of the culture becomes reality to the employees and the supervisor. It is critical that the site manager clearly understands how the supervisor interprets management's objectives and vision for the culture. <u>The visions of upper management become real people doing real things at the supervisor level of the organization.</u> The site manager must create an environment that allows the supervisor to engage and invite contribution. The supervisor must be given that authority.

This must be an environment that allows the supervisor to ask for help from the steward and the workforce. Too often, this is interpreted as a weakness in the supervisor's skill, experience, and courage. If the supervisor has to ask the workforce for help, why do we need the supervisor? If this perception is not changed, it can and will become the driving force behind the supervisor's actions with his or her crew. Survival is a powerful motive and, especially in today's environment, job security can be defined by fear, intimidation, and perception of upper management's expectations.

Affirming the supervisor's right, and yes, even accountability for asking for help, validates the inclusive culture and the working-together model. It cannot be lip service but must be practiced daily, especially at the supervisor level.

The benefits of this approach are both tangible and practical. The shift steward is generally elected by his peers or appointed by the departmental rep or local president. Either way, the individual represents the crew and becomes an important channel of information. Those individuals have usually had the benefit of additional training by the local or international union in areas of negotiation, confrontational skills and contract interpretation. But regardless of training or experience, this individual is the formal leader of the crew as recognized by the union. The site manager or upper management must affirm the supervisor's right to bring the union into the discussion and the process. This is the front lines of the culture. When the invitation to contribute occurs at this level, it has dramatic results. This affirmation cannot be left to perception or assumption by the supervisor. It must be a clear message from management.

The supervisor role must require both leadership and technical capabilities. Although the supervisor must be process capable, it's not necessary that she be the technical expert or that she has all the answers, all the time. A common fault of many organizations is to make the expert the supervisor or leader. When the best welder is the supervisor of the welding crew, yet has no leadership skills, all you have is one less welder. Process capability without leadership skills will not advance the culture or the organization.

PEOPLE: THE REAL BUSINESS OF LEADERSHIP

The story is as old as industry itself. The best welder is promoted to the supervisor of the welding crew. He has no leadership skills, and the people problems begin to create real difficulties within the crew and the business. The crew gravitates to the informal leader of the crew. Eventually, management recognizes the issues and makes the informal leader the assistant supervisor. Another layer of management has been introduced between the worker and upper management and additional costs have been added. To further compound the problems, communication and accountabilities have been further confused. Leaders must have leadership skills first. It's not the supervisor's job to have all the answers all the time.

Combining basic leadership skills and capability with a good working knowledge of the process in an inclusive environment will be a proven platform for success. An environment that allows for joint resolution on issues such as safety, overtime solicitation and assignment, attendance, quality, equipment and process issues will optimize the full capabilities of the organization.

This environment is ideal for promoting this working-together relationship. The shift steward is on the supervisor's team or crew and the two are together daily, optimizing the opportunities for contact. The opportunities are endless for interaction and relationship building. Whether the environment is an office or plant situation, the fundamentals are the same. Just being in the same locale everyday over a long period of time will allow for the natural development of a relationship. The individuals will determine how effective the relationship becomes. A reality of life is that we like some people better than others, and proximity is no guarantee of compatibility. However, we can develop certain ground rules for the working relationship, optimizing the shared objectives of the organization.

The site manager and/or upper management can articulate a vision of the inclusive culture and must practice it at their level in the organization. For it to be real, the vision must become action that can be seen, heard, and felt by the employees during their workday. <u>Nowhere in the organization can this be done more effectively than at the supervisor level.</u> This individual has the opportunity many times every day to turn the vision into action and make the inclusive culture "the way we do things around here." That's powerful and it will produce powerful outcomes for any organization.

Chapter 25:
The Working-Together Platform
(Joint Leadership Meetings)

The working relationships discussed in the preceding chapters become the foundation for a working-together approach to the issues and opportunities of the organization. Those relationships affirm a consistent message to all levels of the organization. Chaos and rumor love a vacuum. Filling the communication vacuum with timely, consistent information will prevent many untruths, perceptions, and rumors.

With the individual relationships between management and union leaders established, the next step is to formalize the approach with a cadence of Joint Leadership Meetings. Those meetings should include the site manager, key staff and the union leadership. A regular pattern of putting those two groups in the same room with an agenda based on relevant information will pay big dividends to the business.

Quarterly is a good frequency and provides for timely updates and feedback on key business goals. In general, issues cannot get too out of control or outdated with a quarterly schedule. Don't have meetings just to have meetings. There has to be relevant information that has value to the business. It also needs to be information that builds trust and sends a strong message of inclusion to the union leadership. Always use discretion and common sense, but err on the side of disclosure as it will build a solid relationship of trust. Giving the group vanilla information that's available to anyone is a waste of time and can be perceived as patronizing and insulting.

A good approach to the agenda is to cascade from general-market and industry information to specific company information followed by site-specific information. This will give the two groups an overall status update. Remember, those are the key leaders in the facility who interact daily with the employees. They will be answering the questions and having the break-room and water-cooler conversations where the question will always be, "How are we doing?" and "Why did we do that?" and "When will we do this?" And the unspoken question for all, "Are we okay and do I still have a future here?"

Information is power, and the right information can empower people in many ways. Being valued enough to be included in the conversation is powerful. This gives people validation, self-respect, and confidence. It also reflects trust and respect. People will get it. Those values and characteristics can now be translated into positive, creative action yielding powerful outcomes for the organization. A well-informed workforce with the proper context can respond in a powerful way and create a competitive advantage. "Check your brain at the gate" has never worked and it never will.

Although safety and process information is always relevant, give serious thought and planning to the financial information included in those meetings. There are laws and corporate governance issues dealing with the disclosure of certain financial information, especially in publicly held companies. Understand those completely and find the legal, appropriate financial information that works for your organization.

The financial information is critical as it is the most commonly questioned or mistrusted area. Management is frequently responding to issues with the "cost" constraint and many times that restraint is used as the convenient excuse why management won't or can't do something related to employee issues. If management never shares the information and the union leadership can only guess or speculate as to the cost issues, it will always be perceived as a smoke-and-mirrors response.

Get the numbers out there. The joint leadership meeting is an excellent forum in which to have a controlled discussion that allows for monitoring understanding and perception of the cost issues. Although certain cost and financial data can be confusing to the workforce as a whole, it can be extremely useful with this smaller group. The group may never completely agree or perceive the issues the same way, but there can at least be an understanding and context of the cost issues for the facility. This creates allies and some level of understanding with the union leadership. This is especially productive as they interact with the larger workforce.

This is where the involvement of the site controller is important. Those meetings are a great opportunity to expose the "finance guy" to the union leadership. When the union leadership knows and trusts the finance guy, the trust of the numbers will follow. If we can all agree on and trust the numbers, we can begin to discuss and explore solutions to issues and opportunities. This trust can only occur with regular exposure to the controller and the numbers. While profit or ebitda numbers may be off limits, cost issues should be discussed and understood by all. Again, err on the side of disclosure. Sharing the good and bad of cost issues will build trust and provide the basis for a platform of joint resolution and improvement.

The other component of this joint meeting is the opportunity to include important company executives external to the site. It's an excellent format to include presentations by the sales, finance, human resources, and operations executives. There are several benefits of those additions to the agenda.

First is the exposure of the executives to the staff and union leadership. It's important for the union leadership to have contact and conversation with those individuals. This reinforces the consistency of the information and assures local leaders the vision expressed by the site manager is a reflection of the company. It's also important for local leaders to know the site manager has the support of the company and the upper management, and it's important for the local leaders to hear those executives express that support and articulate a common vision, strategy, and goal.

The other benefit of this exposure is to build some history of dialogue and discussion. This will pay dividends in the next contract negotiation. If the only time the union leadership hears from upper management is during a negotiation, mistrust will almost always be the default position. Get the executives in front of the local leadership group and build some history of working together. There will still be areas of disagreement, but those disagreements will be based on philosophy, doctrine, or strategy, not mistrust.

Another valuable benefit is the additional understanding and knowledge those executives bring to the table. Understanding customer issues, market movements, and pricing issues from sales gives the local leaders better context of why process or operational priorities exist. This broadens the horizon for the employees and better equips them to deal with challenges within the site.

The same benefit exists with the corporate financial and human resources executives. Get them in front of both the staff and the union leaders. Better-informed employees are better problem solvers. They are more creative and more engaged in the continuous-improvement focus needed in today's globally competitive markets.

Fill the communication vacuum with timely, relevant, and honest information. The joint leadership meeting format is an excellent way to build a strong working together relationship. The benefits are ongoing and become another validation of the inclusive culture, a culture built on trust that will result in powerful and positive outcomes for the organization.

Chapter 26:
Human Resources and the Union

The HR organization is the legal and administrative link to the union and the collective-bargaining agreement. It should also be the anchor and platform on which to validate and nurture the inclusive culture. The same relationship of trust must be developed between the HR manager and local union president that exist with the site manager.

The site manager mandates the inclusive culture and uses a cadence of frequent and open communication with the local union president to actualize the culture. The HR manager must share the vision of the site manager and reinforce the mandated culture in his or her daily actions and the administration of the department.

The HR department is the keeper of the keys in every major area that touches the employee's work life. Most HR departments administer the payroll, insurance and benefit systems, job classification, and bidding and award systems, as well as vacation and attendance systems. The department is also the interpreter of overtime and other work-rules language in the contract. Those have an impact on both the employee's work life and personal life.

One can also draw parallels to those issues and the core union concerns discussed earlier. Because two of the four core concerns are wages-benefits and specific job-ownership issues, then HR is a very direct link in the labor-management relationship. The administration of those issues will have definite impact on the employees' perception of the culture. It's also important to examine the HR department's approach. Is the approach customer-service based or beaurocratic? To fully realize the benefits of the inclusive culture, HR must have a customer-service approach. Most employees are not insurance experts and only concerned with the details when they need the benefit. Payroll, insurance, and retirement benefits get personal and emotional very quickly. A department that responds with concern, empathy, and urgency will build trust and confidence with the workforce. The news may not always be good, but when answers to concerns are delivered with timeliness and a sense of caring, they will pay dividends. Employees will know someone has their back and is watching out for their best interest as well as the company's.

Outsourcing those services is popular today and can result in cost savings through reduction of staff and in-house administration. However, exercise caution when reducing the hands-on, human touch of those services. Those are emotional areas and can present complex, confusing situations.

The demands and challenges of today's businesses require the contributions, experience, and skill of all resources. If the employees are focusing on problems with their pay, their insurance, retirement or other benefit issues, then their energy is not focused on the process, the product, and the customer.

Chapter 27:
Human Resources in the Inclusive Culture

The name of the department speaks for itself. Humans are the most valuable resource of the organization and they should also be the most valued resource of the organization. How do companies demonstrate that value? In the inclusive culture, this value is evident in many areas. The culture lives in the processes, policies, management style, safety programs and in the administration of its human resources practices.

The typical HR department provides several services for the organization, from legal compliance to training. It certainly is the compliance division of the organization as related to local, state, and federal laws. The department must be the expert in legal areas, such as hiring practices, EEO regulations, employee rights, and labor practices for both union and non-union employees.

Is the HR department more effective as part of the legal arm of the organization, or should it stand separate from the legal department? My view is that it should stand alone, separate and without reporting accountabilities to the legal department. The HR manager should report directly to the site general manager, and at the corporate level, there should be a VP of Human Resources reporting directly to the President.

The old saying, "If all you have is a hammer, everything looks like a nail" might apply. If HR reports to legal, then every human resource issue will be examined first from a legal perspective. In that scenario, critical people issues can be overlooked and sub-optimized in order to cover any legal risk embedded in the issue. A "shoot first, ask questions later" mentality will emerge as the pattern and perception of "how things are done around here." And that will not nurture nor confirm the inclusive culture. Instead, it will deprive the organization of heroic gains in productivity, safety, quality and profitability.

Legal has a role in HR, even a major role, given the litigious mentality and the high cost of legal processes, lawsuits, contract arbitrations and lawyer fees. HR must apply the legal filters and tests to many HR issues. However, they cannot be the only filters and tests on issues. HR must remain a stand-alone department, utilizing legal resources as needed but free to make the case for risk analysis and a more people-centered response to issues.

If HR is not a legal arm of management, it can be a customer-service arm of management. Their primary role is to provide the employees with the tools needed to optimize their contribution to the organization. HR is also the gatekeeper of the employee's compensation and benefits packages.

The trend has been to outsource many HR functions, provide a kiosk in a central location and a 1-800 service to get information. Although some HR services can be distributed with those tools, there must be an eye to eye approach to many of the most basic HR services. Payroll, insurance, and retirement issues require a personal touch, an empathetic bedside manner and genuine concern. Those are the issues that people build their lives on, and although they're often debated, those services are associated with the employer. The HR departments will be a strong enabler of the inclusive culture by providing those personal services from a customer-service approach. Again, if employees have to focus on insurance, pay, and other life issues, how can we in management expect them to focus and on the productivity, safety and quality processes?

If the homeless and hungry show up at the back door of the local church, the minister must first fill their belly before he saves their soul. So too must our leaders and HR departments attend to the employees' basic needs before they can expect the employees' full focus and creativity. If we can't fix the insurance or payroll issues and communicate the facts with compassion, interest, and in a timely manner, we will alienate the people and our ability to influence the power of their contributions. It does make a difference.

Right or wrong, people don't separate work issues and life issues. HR doesn't have to provide all the right answers, but they do need to demonstrate that somebody cares and is trying to help. We've heard that people don't want you to solve their problems; they just want you to listen. They want you to listen and demonstrate that you're trying to help find a solution or fix a problem. That's the true test of the culture, behavior that validates that our employees <u>are indeed</u> our most valued resource.

If management is accountable for producing the best possible product or service, then the HR department is a key ally in this objective. The HR department must be a critical enabler to the inclusive culture. This is another reason the HR department should be part of the site manager's staff and not in a direct reporting line to the corporate HR function.

Employees today face many challenges in the workplace. The environment is different on a competitive, social, and cultural level. HR's role in supporting a nurturing environment for training, compliance, and services is critical in today's changing workplace.

Our world is changing, as is the workplace environment. The workplace is a microcosm of the world around us, and we cannot separate the two. Wouldn't it be simple if our employees could deposit all their personal problems in a container at the front door and leave them outside while they put in their day's work? Of course they can't, so we must understand what our workplace environment really is as opposed to what we think it is.

Consider the workplace of today and the issues of change we face in our daily lives. Our businesses and companies are under intense global and domestic competitive pressure. How many of our employees are here today because their previous employer moved operations off shore or shut down? Those employees know firsthand the challenges of global competition. Our employees face that prospect daily and know too well the risk of global competition.

One first-hand example was our Aleris welded-tube division. We built a new plant in the southeast and hired about 50 employees. This plant formed aluminum tube from coiled aluminum and cut it to specific customer-required lengths. Our top customer was a US manufacturer of wind chimes. We shipped aluminum tubes in varying lengths and the customer fabricated, packaged and sold wind chimes to US customers. They soon notified us that his China supplier could ship him pre-fabricated product, packaged and ready for the consumer at a cost cheaper than we could produce the lengths. After a gallant fight, the plant closed less than two years after opening and everyone involved lost their jobs. This is only one of thousands of stories highlighting the global job wars. Employees everywhere and in almost every business live with the threat every day. It is a reality of the workplace today.

At this writing we are in the worst economic crisis since the depression of the 30's. Unemployment is currently at 10.2% and is expected to rise in the first half of 2010. The federal government has bailed out the nation's biggest banks and provided federal money to the big automakers. Foreclosures have decimated the housing market, numerous smaller banks have failed, and hundreds of companies are in bankruptcy. With 72% of the national economy tied to consumer spending, getting people back to work is crucial to the economic recovery.

Times are tough for many people and middle-class America is under siege. Layoffs are the strategy of the day and over 7 million jobs have disappeared. And in many cases, those left in the business face each day wondering whether they are next. If their job is secure, they are most likely doing their work and the work of their laid-off coworkers. It's become a vicious reality as companies continue to shed costs by shedding people. All this makes for a tough day at the office and an even tougher conversation at home. That is the reality of the workplace today. Fear is at a fever pitch in many workplaces today.

The workplace is different in many ways from the corporations a generation ago. One of the strongest ties our fathers had to their companies was the benefits of retirement and insurance. Today, my mother is 84 years old and remarkably, still has basically the same retiree health insurance package my Dad had from his 35 years with General Electric. It has, in many ways, defined her later years. Her financial well being since my dad's passing in 1999 has been assured as a result of GE's choice to continue this wonderful benefit.

That benefit is unique in today's environment of retreating benefits. Retiree medical is all but gone for most salaried employees today and is short-lived for most union contracts, if it can be successfully negotiated out. There's no question those benefits are extremely costly and problematic for most companies, and there have to be workable solutions created. The solution for most, regrettably, is to discontinue them.

The same holds for active employees' health insurance as cost-cutting measures result in increased employee contributions, increased deductibles, higher out of pocket costs, and reduced coverage. For the younger single employee in relatively good health, it isn't a big issue, but for the family with children and chronic health issues, it's both a major reduction of spendable income and an alarming concern about the future of employee health insurance benefits. There are no easy answers, and there are legitimate arguments on both sides of the issue.

Diversity is another changing aspect of today's workplace. Employees work side by side with people of different cultures, races, and backgrounds. Although this is not a new social issue with today's younger generation, it can be challenging for older generations. The X and Y generations have grown up in a different world, and to their credit, have broken down many of the racial and cultural barriers previous generations guarded. Progress is being made on all fronts and in every part of society. The recent election is validation of our social progression, and it confirms the impact of today's younger generation on politics, social reform, and the style of leadership demanded.

Even so, in many workplaces today, the old biases and strains of racial and cultural conflict remain real and active. In many cases, those are issues not always visible to the casual visitor in the facility. Unfortunately, site leaders are also oblivious to those conflicts. Those issues are undercurrents and cancers that are morally wrong but also drain and dilute the productivity, safety and quality of work life.

Employees experience those issues, know where they originate and live with them every day. They occur in our businesses and they are a reality of the workplace today. As site leaders and HR leaders, we must be constantly vigilant in our quest to raise awareness, provide training, and react quickly and firmly to those issues.

Today's employees also come to work with a heightened sense of corporate greed and wage disparity. Even if the employee hasn't had a personal issue with wage discrimination or sees evidence in his or her company of CEO privilege, the awareness is there. The media coverage of CEO excesses and exponentially widening gaps between executive and worker compensation has become water-cooler conversation and common fare on the cable news programs. This issue is amplified by the economic crisis and the highest unemployment rate in decades. When there is a pot in every kitchen and a chicken in every pot, no one gets too excited about CEO pay. People don't like it and it angers them, but if hasn't affected them personally, it's not as big an issue. But when people are hurting and with millions out of work, those excesses by executives are perceived as criminal in nature and the revolution mindset grows with each new tale of CEO and executive extravagance.

There are always differing points of view and no doubt most CEOs and executives work hard every day to add value to their companies and create wealth for their investors. However, I would submit that even in the purest definition of capitalism, it is difficult to justify many of those stratospheric compensation packages. Many cases would suggest the CEO's skill is primarily in manipulating complex financial tools and paper assets. That manipulation and the wholesale genocide of workers in order to raise the paper value of the company is neither the essence nor the genius of leadership. It raises the stock price and some get wealthy. Good for some, but is it worth 400 to 600 times the value of an average worker? Not by most definitions.

Those may not be specific issues in every organization, but the awareness is higher than ever. If its break-room conversation, then it is a reality of the workplace. Perceptions become reality, and that reality becomes a drain on the focus needed to optimize the contribution of all our employees. And <u>that</u> is a reality of the workplace.

Another issue facing employees today is the pending "Employee Free Choice Act" or card check law. This is gaining in popularity and has the support of the current administration and the Democratic congress. It is a hotly debated issue and clearly draws the line between management and labor philosophies.

The law simply says that if 50% + 1 of the employees sign a card expressing a desire to have a union, then you must have a union. No formal vote is required unless the employees choose an election. Under the current law a formal vote must occur to confirm the union status. Unions have argued that management has unfairly used the time before the election to intimidate the workforce through captive audience meetings with anti-union facts, figures, and scare tactics.

Management argues that without the election process, all employees will not be given the opportunity to express their wishes and a small majority of the workforce will determine the fate of all. Regardless of one's belief and persuasion, the legislation is on the table, and in time it will be considered in its present form or in some amended version.

This is not an issue in a unionized facility, but it is a reality for all other businesses, regardless of size. Being small made many businesses off limits for union organizers, but today organized labor is looking at every opportunity to expand its membership and causes. Businesses of all types and sizes are now potential areas of growth for labor. The pending law will invoke heated debate, and it will be an issue in many facilities in the months ahead.

Yes, the environment of today's workplace is changing and challenging. Employees today, regardless of their role or accountability, walk into a socially and politically charged atmosphere every day. How do they deal with those issues, questions, and pressures? What impact do those issues have on the focus of the business? To what degree do they dilute the productivity, safety, quality and creativity of employees and processes? Those are questions leaders must examine and answer. And more importantly, leaders must react and respond to those issues. Those are real issues for people, whether perceived or experienced.

To ignore those people issues in our workplace environment or to wrongly believe the job will be the primary focus is to be naïve and out of touch with the reality of the social process. The fact is that people will do the job as they have through many past challenges. They do it instinctively, by muscle memory, skill and repetition. Many can do their job blindfolded and meet the minimum requirements and specifications day after day. The real focus and brainpower will be on those issues that have an impact on their lives, their families, and their sense of survival.

People can chew gum and walk at the same time. In many jobs, through rote repetition and habit, employees suffer silently in anonymity each day. They get the job done while focusing on those issues outside of their jobs. To lose the creativity and magic of even one human resource is a loss of potential business success and competitive advantage. It's also a waste our businesses can't afford. And in any business, to eliminate waste and optimize all resources is the accountability and the essence of leadership.

The HR department is a vital ally to management in creating an environment that provides the resources, services, and training that unlocks the potential of every employee. That potential exists in everyone, some more than others, but it is there. HR must respond to employees with a professional yet compassionate, empathetic, and caring bedside manner.

Is the employee issue one of training, payroll questions, insurance complexities, or retirement issues? Those are personal and emotional issues that generally have an impact on not only the employee, but also their families. It doesn't get any more personal than that.

Our job as leaders is to allow that potential to materialize. How many of our employees work to live instead of living to work? Have we created workplace environments where most employees just want to get through the day and put in their time, in order to get to the things in life that give them the real fulfillment and joy? It's difficult to glamorize many jobs, but we can and must find ways to unleash the creativity, talent and passion of people.

After work our employees are coaches, community volunteers, church leaders and teachers, small business owners, politicians, craftsmen, parents and spouses. We see only one dimension of those gifted and passionate people. How many leave those passions and gifts at the door each morning? How have we as leaders snuffed out those passions and relegated people to the mundane, constrained confines of the job?

With a customer-service approach in the HR services and a nurturing, inclusive culture, we can create and sustain a workplace environment that will tap into those passions and create a competitive edge for our businesses. People in the right circumstances create powerful outcomes. It happens every day.

Effective leaders make positive changes. Reversing the trend of outsourcing and downsizing HR services will be an investment in our employees and an investment in productivity and performance. Capitalize on the specialty skills available today in the HR disciplines. More than any other area, HR associations provide their professionals with accredited training and certification in every aspect of human services. We must ensure that we have the resources to provide employee training in critical areas of compliance, diversity, benefits and job-specific skills.

Structuring our HR departments to meet those critical needs will be productive and cost effective. With the proper resources, we can design and implement the needed training and administrative services that reinforce the inclusive culture and value employees. The skills, experience, and expertise is available to develop a Human Resources department and strategy that will optimize the creativity, passion, and performance of the entire workforce.

We must also reinvent our relationships with local public schools and community and technical colleges. At the high school level, great opportunity exists to redesign traditional curriculums to more closely meet the needs of our industries and businesses. We must identify those students who choose a different path than the traditional four-year universities. Those students will most likely stay in the area and pursue careers. They will become the foundation of the local economic engine in the community.

Matching those students with programs to better prepare them for the workplace will advance our business community and overall community development. We cannot be afraid or hesitant to break with some traditions. Not only can we provide skills in industrial maintenance and crafts but also in leadership, management and supervisory skills. In heavy industrial locations, there will be critical shortages of those jobs due to aging workforces and the wholesale retirement of baby-boomers. Deliberate programs designed to enable high school or community college graduates to take on those roles quickly will be invaluable to local industries.

Health care jobs will be the number one job opportunity of the next decade. Preparing our high school students as well as displaced workers for those occupations is a critical requirement of our high schools and our technical colleges.

Business and industry HR leaders are natural partners with our educational leaders in planning, designing and implementing those programs. With workforce development as one of the top issues facing the business community, our HR leaders must get involved and lead those discussions. Business cannot sit on the sidelines and be silent in the development, training, and education of its future employees. The long-term cost and risk is simply too high.

Effective and courageous leaders must invest in their HR departments and recognize the value of those professionals as keys to unlocking the power and passion of all employees. Those professionals must also be given the challenge and accountability of the development of their future employees by partnering with local education leaders.

Our employees face a changing workplace. As leaders, we can meet the challenges of those changes with honest communication, updated training and clear expectations. We can also redefine the workplace by developing and nurturing an inclusive, people-centered culture, one that is designed to optimize the contributions of today's employees and embrace our future employees.

Chapter 28:
The Power of People

I grew up as an athlete. My family was immersed in competitive sports from the time I was six years old and my dad took me to my first minor-league tryouts. My dad, E.R. "Russ" Baker, was an Industrial Relations manager with the General Electric Company and he also coached the plant's industrial league baseball and basketball teams. It was incredibly competitive, and the local plants took as much pride in their sports teams as they did in product quality. It was a different time and it seemed no expense was spared in order to field quality teams using quality equipment. For me and my two brothers, it was a continuous adventure. We were the bat boys for the baseball team and the ball and water boys for the basketball teams.

Our exposure to the extraordinary talents and personalities of the players was a continuous education. Our dad was about 5'8', completely fearless and the most focused and passionate man I ever knew. He was confident, stood firmly on his convictions and was respected and admired by all who knew him. I saw in my dad the essence of real leadership, its power, passion, and compassion. It was as natural for him as breathing. When he died at age 86, at his funeral, I saw proof positive of the impact he had on an incredibly wide range of people over his lifetime.

He was never CEO of General Electric, never the most powerful guy in the company or the richest, but he got it right. He was successful many more times than he failed, and he left everything he touched better than when he found it. After 35 years in various management roles with GE, he retired to his small farm where he pursued his second career as a funeral director. At age 70, after serving a three-year apprenticeship at the local funeral home, he passed his state boards and became a licensed funeral director. He shined even brighter when he reached out to people in their darkest hours. He also became a certified EMT and served for twelve years as the assistant coroner for the county while also serving as director of the county's Parks and Recreation Department. He retired again shortly before he became ill. He loved people and he instinctively knew how to bring out the best in everyone he met. He knew the power of bringing people together to reach beyond their grasp. He knew the power of accomplishing great things and not caring who got the credit. And he knew the power that came from doing the right thing. In the final years when he slipped into the darkness of Alzheimer's, his personality and those people-centered traits were still there. His life was defined by serving others, yet he always seemed to be in charge. He was the real deal and the greatest man I ever knew. He was a leader by every definition.

Growing up with this example and immersed in competitive athletics through my college years, I saw many examples of the power of people. I saw how, under the right leadership and in the right environment, kids from little league to college achieved successes greater than their abilities. I saw the power of a common purpose, a common vision, and the outcomes of believing in something bigger than one's self. When I was finished as a player and began a ten-year coaching career, I saw it again and again.

This power of people resulted in more achievements than failures, and not just in win-loss records. I've had the unique opportunity to watch many of those young athletes grow into strong, contributing adults working and raising their families.

Many of them worked for me at the plant and I've seen that same purpose, vision, and belief in the workplace that I saw on the basketball court or baseball field.

The power of people has unlimited potential. When allowed to blossom in the right environment with the right leadership, powerful outcomes follow.

As a young aspiring leader or as a veteran manager who simply has come to believe there is a better way, it is my hope that the values, ideas, and methods in this book have helped you think again on the real essence of leadership.

I don't know for sure whether leaders are born. I've seen many definitions of leadership and most are inspiring and meaningful. If I had to define leadership in a formal definition, it might be this: <u>Leadership, n. The ability to influence people to positive action through a position of respect and credibility for the purpose of achieving a successful outcome.</u>

I do know we all have certain instincts and a capacity to inspire others to action. Those capacities are more evident in some than in others. No one lives in a vacuum or is truly singular in his or her existence. We are all touched by someone and we, in turn, touch others. For those whose capacities to inspire and lead is great, I believe our greatest achievements will come when we as leaders truly believe in the unlimited power of service to the people we lead.

That service will best be defined by using our vested authority as leaders to nurture an inclusive culture that truly unlocks the potential of all the resources in our organization.

The End

Bibliography

Phillips, Donald T. 1992. *Lincoln on Leadership, Executive Strategies for Tough Times.* Warner Books, Inc. New York.

Patterson, R.A. 1992. *New Roget's Thesaurus and Webster's Dictionary.* PSI Associates, Miami, FL.

Jacques, Elliot. 1989. *Requisite Organization: A total system for effective Managerial Organization and Managerial Leadership for the 21st Century.* Cason Hall and Co. Arlington, VA.

McDonald, Ian; Burke, Catherine; Stewart, Carl. 2006. *Systems Leadership: Creating Positive Organizations.* Gower Publishing, Ltd. Hampshire, England.

Hirano, Hiroyuki. 1995. *5 Pillars of the Visual Workplace.* Productivity Press, Portland, Oregon.

www.ingramcontent.com/pod-product-compliance
Lightning Source LLC
Chambersburg PA
CBHW030755180526
45163CB00003B/1034